How To Fix Your Software Project

The plain English guide to IT project turnaround for business leaders and entrepreneurs

Ian Howlett

TABLE OF CONTENTS

About the author 7

Who this book is for 9
About you, 9

Who will benefit most from reading this book? 11
About your situation, 11

Quick-start guide 13

The light at the end of the tunnel 15
If your IT project is failing, you're not the only one!, 15
There is hope!, 16
How you can succeed too, 18

Check if the project is still worthwhile 21
Conclusion: What we achieved in step 1, 26

Determine what you've got to work with 27
Activity 2.1: Map out each part of your project, 29
Activity 2.2: Decide what time, cost, and quality you can work with, 30
Activity 2.3: Decide your tolerances for time, cost, quality, and scope, 31
Conclusion: What we achieved in step 2, 33

Find why your project is currently failing 35
Activity 3.1: Identify the symptoms of failure on your project, 37
Activity 3.2: Identify the reasons your project is failing, 37
Conclusion: What we achieved in step 3, 39

Understand project management for IT projects 41
Find a method to end the madness, 42
PRINCE2: Tells you what should be done, when, and by whom, 44
Activity 4.1: Identify people with project management
and project assurance knowledge, 46
PMP or APMP skills, 47
Agile Development, 48

Activity 4.2: See if agile principles could help you, 53
Agile Principles, 54
Activity 4.3: See if the Agile Manifesto could help you, 55
Agile Manifesto, 55
Conclusion: What we achieved in step 4, 56

How to fix your management problems 59

The project is trying to achieve too much (scope is too wide), 60
Unrealistic expectations, 61
Unarticulated project goals, 62
Wrong people on the project, 63
Marketing failure, 63
Inadequate support from leaders and upper management, 65
Poor reporting of the project's status, 66
Inaccurate estimates of needed resources, 67
Stakeholder politics and lack of stakeholder consent, 70
Commercial pressures, 71
Built the wrong thing to solve the business problem, 72
Poor user training and documentation, 73
Failure to proactively manage risk, 76
Wrong decision to build software vs customizing an existing package, 83
People are trying to do too many things at the same time, 90
Lack of open discussion with third parties concerning budget, 95
Conclusion: What we achieved in step 5, 98

How to fix your IT skills problems 99

Badly defined requirements, 100
Changing requirements that are not handled correctly, 103
Low level of customer/user involvement, or involvement too late, 105
Poor communication among customers, developers, and users, 106
Use of the wrong technology
(immature, outdated, not fit for purpose), 109

Poor development practices, 110

Poor software testing, 113

Poor reporting and handling of bugs and defects, 120

Inability to handle the project's complexity, 126

Conclusion: What we achieved in step 6, 127

Get the right people on the project 129

You: The senior leader, entrepreneur, or executive, 130

Developers, 131

Testers, 137

Project manager, 138

Project assurance, 139

Conclusion: What we achieved in step 7, 140

Keeping a promise 141

The one true silver bullet for successful software projects , 141

The million dollar secret behind keeping your project continually focused on success, 142

How to piggyback on the knowledge gained from thousands of successful projects, 142

The 26 major root causes of software project failure... and how to fix them, 143

The #1 personal quality you'll need in order to succeed, 143

The insider's trick to having software that doesn't suck, 143

Final Thoughts, 144

About the author

Ian Howlett works with companies to achieve measurable business results from their software projects.

He has an MBA with distinction from the University of Oxford, a bachelor's degree in computer science, and is a certified PRINCE2 practitioner in project management.

He has worked extensively as a software developer, business analyst and project manager, for or with leading companies large and small, including Unisys (IT systems integration), BUPA (healthcare), FT.com (financial media), TMSC (travel insurance), and easyJet, a major European airline.

His interests include playing the piano, motor racing, and piloting light aircraft. He has a Private Pilot's Licence. He lives with Victoria and two naughty cats called Tom and Jerry.

How to Contact the Author

You may contact the author through his private office, by sending an email to info@ianhowlett.com.

····················

Who this book is for

About you

I wrote this book to be a friendly and accessible guide for the people I work with most often: business leaders, entrepreneurs, and employees who are trying to make IT projects a success.

That means that you're likely to be a company founder, company owner, CEO or Managing Director, or a manager within a larger organisation.

If you report directly to one of these people you're likely to find this book useful too.

You're likely to have a company of between 5 and 250 employees, although you could well have more or fewer.

This isn't a book written for technical people, although that's the background I come from, and it's a role I continue to perform myself from time to time. However, technical people will also find this book useful, as a checklist of things to do, and to gently point clients in the right direction where required.

You'll notice that this book isn't a huge thick doorstop: I value your time, so I've kept things concise and to the point.

Who will benefit most from reading this book?

About your situation

The advice I give in this book is general good advice, and can be applied to almost any IT project. However, you're likely to find it most useful if:

1. Your project is strategically important.
2. A lot is at stake and your project must come out right.
3. Your project has started but is going wrong: is over time or over budget, or software is poor quality.
4. You feel your project is currently heading more towards disaster than triumph!

You will be doing one or more of the following things:

1. Customising an existing software package to fit your needs; often known as Commercial Off-The-Shelf (COTS) software.
2. Building your own software in-house.
3. Building your own software by working with a software development company.

Bear in mind that I know nothing about you or your company personally (unless you choose to work with me), so I can't take responsibility for your actions or your results.

Quick-start guide

A lot of books sit on shelves and never get read. I want you to get maximum value from this book, even if you've only got five minutes right now, which is why I'm giving you this summary. I really want you to get your project back on track and give it your best shot.

This book is very light on theory, and there's no management-speak mumbo-jumbo either. That's not my style. I won't leave you floundering around, wondering what to do next. This is a straight-talking set of seven simple and practical steps that you can start using immediately. In each step I'll give you a clear list of actions to take to get you closer to success.

To be successful, you'll need to take practical action. To help you with that, I've given you some activities throughout each step. I strongly recommend that you work through all of these activities.

At the end of each step I've given you a summary of what you should have achieved.

If you're in a hurry, you can skip straight to steps 5 and 6. I don't recommend it, but if time is tight then that's where you'll find the real meat!

Here's how the book is broken down:

Introduction: I give you a few facts and figures to show that if your project is failing you're far from being the only one! I also point out the good news that help is at hand, and give you some examples of wildly successful projects that I've personally been involved in, to show that success is certainly within your grasp.

Step 1: Check if the project is worthwhile. We'll take a look at your business case, and decide whether to continue with the project or put it out of its misery!

Step 2: Determine what you've got to work with. We'll map out the main areas of your project, and understand the time, cost and quality requirements you'll be working within.

Step 3: Find why your project is currently failing. We'll investigate the main root causes of failure in IT projects, which break down into management problems and IT skills problems. I'll ask you to choose the problems you think you are currently experiencing, so that we can start to address them.

Step 4: Understand project management for IT projects. While this isn't a book about project management, project management failures often have a lot to do with IT project failure, so we'll look at this in a little more depth, and I'll suggest some techniques that will help you.

Step 5: How to fix your management problems. In this step we take a more detailed look at each common management problem in turn, and I'll give you some pointers on how you can fix it.

Step 6: How to fix your IT skills problems. I then focus your attention on specific IT issues, and look again at each one in turn, giving you practical steps to take to turn things around.

Step 7: Get the right people involved. People are crucial to success in IT projects. I'll explain who you really need to have with you to stand a good chance of success.

Now let's get to work!

The light at the end of the tunnel

If you're reading this book, I'm guessing that you're a serious business person with an important IT project that's heading south, and you need to turn it around fast. If that's you, then take the time to read every word of this book, and I'll show you how you can dig yourself out of the hole and *actually get the results* you thought you were going to be getting in the first place.

The benefits of a great IT project can be incredible, and can truly transform your company. You could cut your costs in half, or open up a whole new marketing channel and triple your revenues … or get totally stressed out with a project that just isn't coming up with the goods.

If your IT project is failing, you're not the only one!

The truth is, depending on how you define failure, most studies report that between 30% and 70% of all IT projects fail. That's worse than the survival rate for open heart surgery!

Here's a few statistics on project failure that add up to a horror show. (They're a bit old, but I doubt they've changed much.)

- McKinsey & Company, in conjunction with the University of Oxford, found in 2012 that 17% of large IT projects go so badly wrong that they can threaten the very existence of the company.

- In 2010, KPMG in New Zealand found that a massive 70% of organisations have suffered at least one project failure in the prior 12 months. Beyond this, 50% of people who responded to their survey said that their project failed to consistently achieve what it set out to achieve.

- IBM found in 2008 that only 40% of projects met their goals for time, cost and quality.

- Logica found in 2008 that 35% of organisations abandoned a major project in the last 3 years.

So it seems like most people are having trouble with their IT, they have been struggling for years, and you're truly *not* alone.

There is hope!

But despite these setbacks across the industry, some IT projects *do* go right, and they *do* deliver the benefits that they are supposed to achieve: on time, on budget, and to the right quality. They save costs, they boost revenues, and they increase profits.

Now for the good news: if 70% of projects fail, that means that 30% of projects are a success! That's actually quite a lot of light at the end of the tunnel, if you can just figure out how to get to it, and cut out the mistakes that quickly confine most people to the failing 70%.

By following the exact steps that I'm going to show you in this book, you can dramatically increase your chances of being in the 30% of successful projects.

How do I know this? Because these successful projects are the projects that I have personally worked on during my 15 years in the IT industry. I've seen for myself, first hand, how:

- A major airline was able to add hundreds of millions of dollars per year to its revenues by using software to price its flights according to supply and demand… with a software team of just 4 people.

- A spin-off project from the first airline project was able to add a further $21m per year to revenues by tweaking an existing system, which only needed a team of 3 people for 3 months.

- A travel insurance company was able to perform over 2 million medical screenings, over a course of 5 years, with a software team of just 2 people and with almost no maintenance required.

- A major global publishing firm was able to move from free content to a paid content model that became hugely profitable.

- A startup media company was able to go from dreaming up an idea for a new collaborative publishing platform, then get it to market in only 4 weeks and acquire over 13,000 Facebook fans in 2 months with minimal effort and cost.

That's just a few random examples I chose off the top of my head, to show you some very different projects that I can absolutely assure you from my own personal knowledge have succeeded wildly. I did this to illustrate that *IT projects can and do succeed*, for the largest companies in the world, the smallest companies in the world, and the vast majority of small and medium sized businesses in between: *for companies just like yours.* In other words, whatever size of company you are running, people just like you are succeeding with IT projects.

How you can succeed too

No matter what size of company you're in, and no matter what industry you're in, you *can* bring home the bacon with a great IT project, by using the little-known but effective techniques I'll be showing you in this book.

Just to get you in the right frame of mind, take a moment to imagine what your company would be like if your failing IT project – that millstone round your neck – could be made to work.

Imagine what success would allow you to do. How would it transform your company? What would it do for your results? What would it do for you *personally*? Could you take that round-the-world trip you've been promising yourself?

Before we start, let me tell you a story about one of my private clients: the owners of a mid-sized insurance firm based in Australia. A couple of years ago they decided to open up a new strand of their business, selling policies online. They engaged a firm of software developers who just couldn't come up with the goods and produce working software. Out of pocket, they looked elsewhere, and brought in a new development team who didn't fare much better! Things were looking pretty grim, and funds were getting low. They were close to quitting.

Fortunately, one of my existing clients introduced them to me, and we got chatting. I took them through the *exact series of steps* I'm going to show you here, first to diagnose where they were going wrong, and then to give them a prescription for success.

They're now *profitably* selling online to the public, adding layers of distributors and getting price aggregators to sell for them.

All it took was a bit of good advice to start, bringing the right people onto the team, and then some continued guidance to ensure continued success. In other words, a good nudge in the right direction to get them going, with effective and consistent follow-up to keep them on the right track.

I hope you can see that if they can succeed at turning round their project, then you can succeed too.

So let me show you exactly what I showed them.

Check if the project is still worthwhile

Abraham Lincoln once said, "Give me six hours to chop down a tree and I will spend the first four sharpening the axe". He was referring to getting properly prepared for action. So let's sharpen your axe.

Before you originally started your project, you had some sort of end goal in mind. Maybe that was to launch a website so that you could sell products internationally, or to bring in new warehouse management software to cut costs and reduce inventory, etc. Let's start by looking at this more closely.

Activity 1.1 – List your project's benefits at the time the project first started

Cast your mind back to before the messy business of actually doing the project began, and think about what you initially set out to achieve. Don't worry if the project is in poor shape right now: for this activity, just assume I'm waving a magic wand and the project will come out just fine.

So think about *what you actually want*, not what you think you can currently salvage!

Grab a pen and paper, or fire up Microsoft Word, and list the high level business benefits that you were hoping to achieve with your project.

Make each benefit specific and measurable. I'll give you some examples in a moment which will make this clear.

Remember, don't cast judgment yet on whether you think these benefits are achievable. This is your wish list as it stood when you started the project.

You don't need to spend too long doing this. The first things that come into your head if I ask you "Why are you doing this project?" are usually good enough. Aim to write between 1 and 5 benefits.

Here are some examples based on various different projects I have worked on – you'll soon see the pattern of how you should be writing these benefits here.

- Reduce the number of calls to the call centre by 20%
- Sell $200,000 of products online within the first year of launch
- Increase total company revenues by 10%
- Increase renewals from 50% to 70%
- Enable sales through a network of 1,000 distributors
- Cut costs in the maintenance department by $2m per year
- Reduce industrial plant hire costs from $1.5m per year to $0.5 per year
- Cut to zero the number of workers whose qualifications expire without us realising

So go ahead and write down the benefits you were originally hoping to achieve.

Activity 1.2 – What benefits do you need now?

Now we'll look at each of these benefits in turn, and see if each benefit is still worthwhile, based on where your business is *right now*, not at the point you started the project.

Maybe the benefit would still be great. Maybe the benefit is not needed any more because your commercial world has changed. Maybe the general idea of the benefit is still valuable, but the numbers aren't quite right any more (that's why I asked you to make each of your listed benefits specific).

So here's what I want you to do in this activity:

Take each of the benefits you listed in the previous activity, and write underneath it a changed version, if a change is required, so that it reflects what you need to achieve now to move your company forward.

Again, don't water this down based on whatever state your project is in right now: we'll get to that later. For now just assume that we can fix the project, and decide what your ideal project would give you.

For each benefit, you might choose to leave it completely unchanged, or adjust the numbers to measure the benefit, or just note that the benefit is now completely not needed and wouldn't help your company any more.

I'll give you a worked example, so you can see what to do.

Let's take the first of my example benefits from the list above, "Reduce the number of calls to the call centre by 20%", and explore how three different fictional companies might evaluate it, based on the commercial environment they now find themselves in. (In real life, the evaluation is usually a bit more subtle than I've presented it here, but I've chosen quite obvious examples so that you can see what we're doing here.)

For **Company 1**, this benefit of reducing calls by 20% is still absolutely what's needed. They need to reduce the number of calls to the call centre and a 20% reduction is just enough to bring the call centre back to maximum efficiency.

For **Company 2**, since the start of the project they have experienced a strong rise in the cost of running their call centre. These increased costs have been due to changing their call centre outsourcing partner, and also rising wage and telecommunications costs. In this case, they still want to reduce the number of calls, but now they need to reduce them by 50%, not 20%.

For **Company 3**, since the start of this project they have taken a strategic decision to switch away from a call centre all together, and move to online-only support, delivered via their website. Because of this, reducing calls by 20% is irrelevant, because there won't be any calls at all!

Here's how our three example companies from above would approach this activity:

Company 1:
ORIGINAL: Reduce the number of calls to the call centre by 20%
OK, no change required

Company 2:
ORIGINAL: Reduce the number of calls to the call centre by 20%
NEW: Reduce the number of calls to the call centre by 50%

Company 3:
ORIGINAL: Reduce the number of calls to the call centre by 20%
This benefit is no longer relevant.

So take each of the benefits you listed in the previous activity, and write underneath it a changed version, if a change is required, so that it reflects what you need to achieve now in order to move your company forward.

Activity 1.3: Kill the project, or continue to greatness?

Now let's look at what you've written in the previous activity. This is where some people get their first moment of clarity as to what is going wrong in their project.

If you haven't had to make any changes, like Company 1, and all your benefits are still just what you need, then you're in a good position.

If you've had to make a few changes, like Company 2, then the project that you initially set up could well be failing because it's trying to deliver something that is completely unsuited to the commercial environment you're now in. In this example, we'd probably need to do something drastically different to reduce calls by 50% rather than 20%. If this describes your situation, you need to take a step back and fully recognise this fact. Knowing that drastic change is required can be quite a mind-shift when you're deep into the project, so take some time for this fact to fully sink in.

Company 3 found that its original benefit of reducing the number of calls was no longer relevant. If that was the *only* benefit of their project then of course the project would be shut down. In practice there might be other benefits from the project that are still worth having.

If you find that *all* your benefits are no longer needed then it's time to just abandon your project all together. Don't be afraid to give it the swift sword! Chalk this one up to experience, salvage what you can, and learn whatever lessons you can. You might then need to think of new benefits, start a new project, and put better structures in place to give yourself a better chance of succeeding.

You'd think this would be so obvious that I wouldn't need to tell you, but people often get hung up on their pet projects, can't clearly see that the benefits aren't worth having or will never be reached, or sometimes they're just so engrossed in the detail that they never consider the big picture and realise that ultimately their work will be futile. The practical advice here is just to make sure that you keep an awareness of your overall strategy, even when you're right down in the details.

So for this activity, just take a hard look at your new benefits, and decide whether they would help your business if you could achieve them. If you can't honestly say that the benefits are worth having, end your project now.

If you still want the benefits, then great, let's move onto the next step and see how we can get your project back on track to give you those benefits.

Conclusion: What we achieved in step 1

If you've completed these activities you should now understand the measurable benefits that your project is trying to deliver, and you should know that the benefits are actually worthwhile having. This is a great roadmap to build upon, which is what we'll do in step 2.

STEP 2

Determine what you've got to work with

Now that you've checked and convinced yourself that the benefits of your project are worth having, mentally reaffirm your commitment to achieving those benefits, and visualise what they would mean for your company. This will keep you motivated, and make you realise just how worthwhile the remaining steps are going to be for you.

Since your project is already underway, no matter what state it's in, it's going to have taken up some time and some money, have achieved some level of quality (even if that's just really bad quality), and attempted to actually produce something. That's what we'll look at now.

To put this another way, this step is all about the trade-off between four things:

- **Time**: How long has it taken?
- **Cost**: How much have you spent?
- **Quality**: How good is the software you've created?
- **Scope**: What things have you been trying to do?

You're probably aware of the old saying: "You can have it good, fast or cheap: pick any two." This is really saying that if you want something good (quality) and fast (time), it's not going to be cheap (cost). Alternatively, you can have it cheap, but it can either be good or delivered fast, but not both.

What this phrase ignores though is scope, and scope means deciding which things you are going to do, and which things you are not going to do.

Here's a vital fact to understand on the subject of scope:

One of the biggest causes of IT project failure is that the project tries to do too much.

Trying to do too much—setting the scope too wide—is the single biggest cause of IT project failure that I have seen. Certainly the projects and companies that I've seen close-up that haven't been successful have bitten off more than they could chew, and have been doomed from day 1: beaten before they even started.

But forewarned is forearmed, and I have now forewarned you!

If you look at any government IT project that has failed (and there's certainly no shortage of them to choose from), almost certainly you will quickly see that they tried to do too much. Doing too much spreads the people and money too thinly: quality suffers, and the whole thing becomes an unmanageable mess. Doing too much adds complexity, and complexity is the sworn enemy of software success.

The government approach to IT project failure is usually to lie about it, insist that everything is fine, call anyone who disagrees "unhelpful", and then a few years later scrap the whole project, after wasting a billion dollars or more of taxpayers' money, with nothing to show for it.

Don't be like the government here!

The important thing to realise is that time, cost, quality, and scope are all completely interlinked. Changing one means changing the others.

To give an obvious example, reducing the scope—not doing as much—means that you can either complete the work more quickly, and/or more cheaply, and/or to higher quality. That's usually a good thing.

Activity 2.1: Map out each part of your project

This should be quite a straightforward activity. What we're doing here is defining the scope of your project: what are all the things that you're currently trying to do in the project?

All I want you to do is draw a diagram, like the one I'll show you below, and list the major parts of your project. If it's a website, you might start by breaking down the site into the customer-facing sales part and the admin part. You might then break this down again into a second layer, so the customer part of the site has a product catalogue, a cart, and a payment interface, while the admin part has catalogue admin, order admin, and payment admin.

Go two or three layers deep, and you'll probably end up with between 5 and 30 parts that make up your project, depending on how complicated it is.

Pen and paper is good enough for this, but if you're looking for a good, free tool to produce this diagram on your computer, I recommend **XMind**, which you can get from http://www.xmind.net. It works on PC or Mac and produces mind-maps, which you can quickly format into whichever style you wish. It's a very useful tool for a whole variety of uses throughout your business.

To show you what we're looking for, here's an example scope diagram showing an insurance sales website. You'll see that most of the branches of this tree could be broken down into much more detail, but we don't need to do that here.

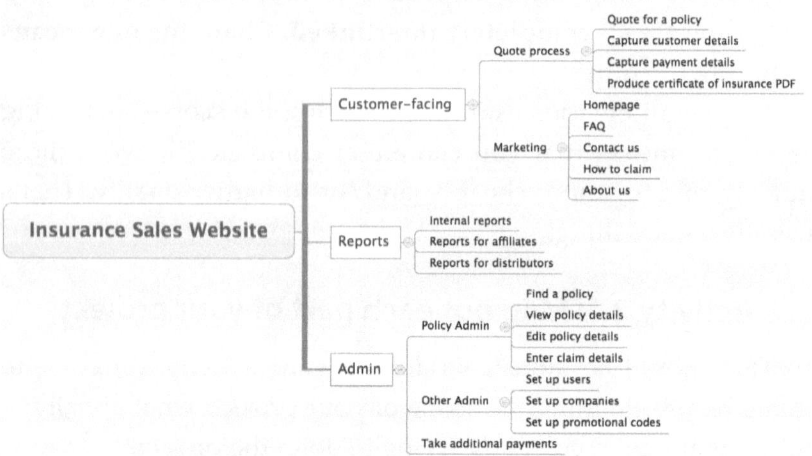

Figure 1. A scope diagram of an insurance sales website, listing the main sections of the site and the tasks the site must perform.

Activity 2.2: Decide what time, cost, and quality you can work with

If you cast your mind back to the benefits that you identified for your project in step 1, we can now start to make sure that the benefits you're going to get are realistic and achievable by seeing what time, cost, quality requirements and scope you've got to accomplish your task with. To exaggerate, we're going to make sure that you're not trying to get a rocket ship to Mars by this time next week.

So it's time to get writing again. Now that you've drawn your project diagram to get an idea of the scope of your project, there are three remaining things I want you to note. So start a separate page—this should only take one page—and write down:

Time: How much time have you got before you need to get at least some benefit from the project? How much time have you got before you need to get all the benefit? For example, if your project is an e-commerce website, it's probably better to get a simple site launched in 2 months and then spending 10 months improving it while it's selling products for you, rather than waiting 12 months before launching anything.

Cost: How much budget do you have remaining that you can make available during the time frame you have just identified? You'll have more stability, so a better chance of success, if this budget is sitting as cash ready to spend, rather than being a speculative amount based on money you only think you're going to be collecting from customers during the course of the project.

Quality: This can sometimes be hard to define, but are you going for a Rolls Royce product, that's totally amazing in every way, or are you willing to define "good enough" at a lower level than this? For example, I've worked on websites where the customer-facing sales part of the site looks great and works really well, but the behind-the-scenes admin interface looks really quite rough (but is good enough to do the job). The site was deliberately engineered to different quality requirements in these different components, so that we could spend more of the time and money where it would make more difference to customers. For now, just get a general idea of the sort of quality you are aiming for.

Activity 2.3: Decide your tolerances for time, cost, quality, and scope

The next thing we're going to do is decide how much tolerance there is in each of these four areas. In other words, are your targets completely fixed, or could we change them a bit to make things easier for ourselves?

So, get your pen out again, and prepare to make some changes:

Time: Do you have to meet a certain date, for example if a regulator or law says that you have to be compliant by a specific date? Or could you finish a few weeks or months earlier or later? If you are flexible on your time target, note down your tolerance. For example, if you've initially written down 12 months, perhaps you could put "+/- 2 months", meaning that really you are happy to take between 10 and 14 months. Just write "zero tolerance" if you can't or won't compromise on time.

Cost: Do you have a fixed budget to work with? Can you spend more, or less, if you had to? Most projects can spend less, but perhaps you could go a bit higher on cost if you needed to. For example, if you think the project will generate $2m per year in profits, whether you spend $300k or $350k – assuming you've got the cash – still gives a great return on investment. Note down your maximum and minimum budget tolerance, for example "+/- $100k".

Quality: In the activity above I gave you the example of a website where the customer-facing part looked great, but the admin part (that only internal employees saw) deliberately didn't have as much attention lavished on it. The point I was making is that not every part of your project has to be perfect in every way in order for the project to be a success. Take the project diagram that you created in Activity 2.1 and score each of the boxes with marks out of 10 for quality, where 1 is a very rough effort that just about does the job, and 10 is as perfect as you can get it. So you might score the customer-facing part as a 9, and the admin part as a 3. Quality has many facets though: graphic design, number of features supported, how well errors are handled, etc. For now though, just give each area a single score out of 10 for how great it would have to be in order to succeed.

Scope: Keep your focus on your project diagram. The reason I just asked you to score each area for quality is that you might find that some areas – likely to be the areas that scored lower on quality – can actually just be cut from the project: either removed permanently or at least cut for now and deferred to some point in the future. So take a look and see if there's anything that actually you could do without. This is really the 80-20 rule in action: you'll probably get 80% of the benefits of the project with just 20% of the features (or 70-30, or similar). So mark any areas on your diagram that you think your project could do without, at least for now. Remember, one of the biggest causes of IT project failure is trying to do too much, so if you can reduce the amount of things you're trying to do then you'll have a much better chance of success, and you can allocate your time, cost, and ability to produce higher quality across a smaller and more focused number of things. There's a saying in software development, YAGNI: "You Ain't Gonna Need It". This means that if you are developing things just because they might possibly be useful, you should just defer them for now, and focus your efforts on things you're definitely going to need. I've often seen that features we decide to cut from a project turn out to actually never be required, so it's almost always better to under-develop than over-develop.

Conclusion: What we achieved in step 2

If you've completed these activities, you should now understand the time, cost, and quality that you will need to work to in order for your project to be a success. You will also understand how you can flex the time, cost and quality up and down in order to help solve your current problems. You've also looked at the scope of your project, and it's great if you've identified some things to cut from your project to lighten your load.

This is the second part of your road map to success. In step 3, we'll change gear and look at why your particular project is going wrong.

Find why your project is currently failing

In steps 1 and 2 we stayed positive, and focused on the benefits you want to reach, and the resources you've got to get you there. Now we're going to turn to the dark side, and look at project failure, so that we can figure out how to move you past it.

What is failure, anyway? Personally, I'd say that the definition of failure is quite obvious, and it's probably the same as your definition:

A project has failed if it doesn't deliver the expected business benefits.

I'd also go one step further and add some secondary tests: **a project has failed if it doesn't deliver the expected business benefits, when you factor in time, cost, and quality.**

In other words, if it didn't give you the benefits you were expecting, took too long, cost too much, or wasn't fit for purpose, then it either fully or partially failed!

There's a bit of judgment needed in this definition though. Let's look at an example outside of IT to prove this point. When construction started on the Sydney Opera House in 1959, it was estimated to cost $7 million and take 4 years to build. It was finally completed in 1973 and cost over $100 million! But it has since gone on to be a huge success. In this case it delivered the benefits, just not within time and cost. So maybe it's really the estimates that were wrong! (Hey, it really wouldn't be the first time an estimate was wrong!) This example really does need a long-term view though, since at the time of construction nobody would have known the success and acclaim the Opera House would go on to achieve.

Also, the initial expectations have to be reasonable. If the project called for a city on the moon by the end of the month then anyone would fail to deliver this, because it's just not a realistic expectation.

Another way to look at failure is to say that a project failed if it didn't deliver a suitable Return on Investment (ROI). Although looking at the ROI is very useful, it requires a longer-term view, over the full length of time that it will take to gain the benefits of the project, and for this reason it's usually impossible to judge whether an IT project is a success or failure in ROI terms until long after the project has been completed, or it has moved into maintenance mode.

Here's the acid test: whichever way you cut it, if you feel in your bones that the project has failed then it probably has!

So if that's what failure looks like, what are the reasons for failure? One of the most boring things you can ever do is research the reasons why IT projects fail! Trust me, I've done it!

I'll keep the rest of this step nice and short, so that I don't bore you to death, but it's important that you know *why* studying the reasons that projects fail is so boring: because **all projects fail for the same basic reasons!**

Time and time again, in study after study, you see the same reasons for failure coming up. Quite honestly, if airlines were as bad at learning the safety lessons from plane crashes as business people and IT people are at learning the lessons from failed IT projects, then I guarantee you'd never set foot on a plane again!

Activity 3.1: Identify the symptoms of failure on your project

This activity is very simple. Here's a summary of the six major areas in which your project could be exhibiting the signs and symptoms of failure. I've kept the list general, so that you can interpret it with your own project in mind.

Look at the list, and tick each symptom of failure that you think applies to your project right now.

Symptoms of failure

- **Time**: Taking too much time
- **Cost**: Costing too much money
- **Quality**: Quality is too poor in one or more areas
- **Scope**: Trying to do too much and not achieving enough
- **Benefits**: Business benefits not being achieved
- **Risks**: Risks not managed and out of control

Activity 3.2: Identify the reasons your project is failing

I'm about to give you a checklist of common factors in IT project failure. These are the root causes of the symptoms you have just identified. I've loosely broken them down into two major areas: management failures and IT project skill failures.

You'll notice that these categories are quite broad. That's intentional, so that you can read into them whatever comes to mind for your own project. I'm sure that you can see that whole books can (and have) been written on each of these bullet points. You should take heart from that, because it means that once we diagnose the specific reasons for failure, there is a significant established body of knowledge that we can bring to bear to fix the problems.

Most of the management problems are really concerned with the discipline of **Project Management**. We'll come back to that, but I just wanted to make sure you notice it now.

All I want you to do in this activity is just put a tick against the reasons for failure that you think *definitely* apply to your project, and put a question mark against the reasons that you think *might* apply to you. Don't over-think it or worry about the precise wording for now, just go on your gut feeling, which is usually pretty accurate.

Most studies into failed IT projects show that there are multiple reasons for failure, not just one reason. So you should expect to be choosing several or more of these root causes of failure as applying to your own project.

Root causes of failure: Management problems

1. Poor project management
2. Project is trying to achieve too much (scope is too wide)
3. Unrealistic expectations
4. Unarticulated project goals
5. Wrong people on the project
6. Marketing failure
7. Inadequate support from leaders and upper management
8. Poor reporting of the project's status
9. Inaccurate estimates of needed resources
10. Stakeholder politics and lack of stakeholder consent
11. Commercial pressures
12. Built the wrong thing to solve the business problem

13. Poor user training and documentation

14. Failure to proactively manage risk

15. Wrong decision to build software vs customizing an existing package

16. People are trying to do too many things at the same time

17. Lack of open discussion with third parties concerning budget

Root causes of failure: IT skills problems

18. Badly defined requirements

19. Changing requirements that are not handled correctly

20. Low level of customer/user involvement, or involvement too late

21. Poor communication among customers, developers, and users

22. Use of the wrong technology (immature, outdated, not fit for purpose)

23. Poor development practices

24. Poor software testing

25. Poor reporting and handling of bugs and defects

26. Inability to handle the project's complexity

Conclusion: What we achieved in step 3

In step 3 you've taken a first look at why your project might have failed. Hopefully this has got you thinking. If you just went away and tackled each of the root causes you've identified here you'd be well on the road back to success. So in steps 4, 5 and 6 I'm going to give you some concrete action points for how you can tackle each of the root causes of failure, to get you back on track quickly.

Understand project management for IT projects

In step 3 you identified the general problem areas that your project is probably suffering from. If you were a private client of mine, and I was working one-on-one with you to turn around your IT project, we'd look a little more deeply into this list, and go deeper into what you're experiencing and why it has happened. So we can do some very useful work here, and get you on the road to success, just by looking at the items in the list that affect you.

In step 3, you most likely chose "Poor project management" as one of the factors affecting your project—and if you didn't choose it, you probably should have done! It's such a common cause of failure that in this step we're going to look at project management as it applies to successful IT projects, and make sure you've got what you need to succeed.

Find a method to end the madness

Rather than just randomly deciding on things to do, and when to do them, it helps to use an established approach for managing your project and developing your software. We call this approach a "project management methodology".

There are quite a few project management methodologies to choose from, and this is an area that's riddled with dogma and almost religious fervour when it comes to championing certain methodologies and rubbishing others. Be aware that no matter what I write in this section on methodologies, and no matter who was writing this section, there would be a long line of people queuing up to say that everything here is wrong, and there's a much better way of doing it. Of course, a lot of these people have a vested interest of some sort in preserving their own methods, or a commercial interest in selling a specific approach! Never underestimate the power of these vested interests! (My own personal vested interest, as a software success expert, is just making sure you actually get the benefits that your IT project is supposed to be giving you, and beyond that I really don't care how we achieve it!)

The real truth, as I've experienced it for myself, is that there are lots of ways to approach an IT project and get to success. It's truly a case of horses for courses: you need something that fits your size of project and your natural inclination for how you like to work.

The reason that different methodologies are hotly promoted, and have their sworn followers, is that a lot of the methodologies *do* actually work in a lot of cases, *if* you follow them properly *and* you have good people on the project. This explains the fierce debate over which methodology is best, because there's evidence of success and failure in whichever methodology you choose.

Personally, I'd just advise you to choose a methodology and stick to it, but make sure you've got good people to help you.

Good people can mostly save the day no matter what methodology you use. (Likewise, bad people will ruin you no matter what methodology you use.)

Let me explain three useful methodologies, or sets of knowledge, or whatever you want to call them, that I have personally used in projects which between them have delivered well over $500m of revenue.

My aim in this section is just to give a broad overview, to prepare you for the more detailed discussion of project failures that we'll have in step 5. You might well have come across some of these ideas before, perhaps just as buzzwords, perhaps in more depth. But in case this is a new area for you, I'll give you a quick tour of what's available, and why it's going to help you to get your IT project back on the road to success.

The following figure outlines what I'll be showing you in this step. Some people might differ with the summary descriptions I'm giving here, but that's all a bit academic. In the real world, this is what you need to know.

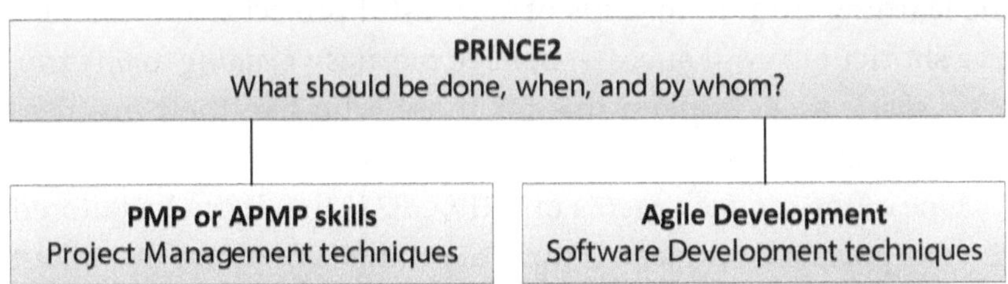

Figure 2. Three key components of IT project management.

PRINCE2: Tells you what should be done, when, and by whom

PRINCE2 is a project management methodology and certification offered by a company called Axelos.

When a lot of people who aren't really familiar with PRINCE2 hear about it, they think of it as some kind of heavyweight, lumbering steamroller that slows everyone down, or something that's old-fashioned and not suited to modern software production. *Nothing could be further from the truth.*

PRINCE2 gives a set of techniques to use on pretty much any type of project, from building a bridge to building a website. It's not just for IT projects. It restricts itself to the business of managing the project itself, not the individual specialist tasks, and tells you what to do, when to do it, and who should be doing it. It defines a full set of roles and responsibilities, to make sure you don't miss out on doing anything important, and it defines a small yet comprehensive series of reports to make sure everything stays on track.

Really, PRINCE2 just takes away the uncertainty about what you should be doing, and in a lot of cases **it's uncertainty that kills projects**.

A huge number of people have spent decades thinking about the material that ended up going into PRINCE2, and it represents the learning from thousands of successful projects, so think of it as a shortcut to your success! Believe me, *it isn't adding complexity, it's a shortcut*. To explain this for those who like their business buzzwords, it means you're not having to reinvent the wheel.

One of the main elements of PRINCE2 is that it can be tailored to your particular project. If there are things you don't like about the methodology, or don't need, then you just choose not to do them! You don't even have to create long and boring documents, you can just do most of it with emails.

It's actually quite easy to learn PRINCE2, even though at first it looks a little overwhelming. There are thousands of people certified in it, and it's used all around the world, so you can find a lot of people who understand it and can apply it. There's a PRINCE2 Successful Candidate Register, to verify credentials, at https://www.axelos.com/successful-candidates-register.

A two day training course can give you the basics of PRINCE2, a five day course can give you all you need to know, and you can even buy audio courses for just a few dollars that will teach you everything. I personally like the PRINCE2 courses at Management Plaza, given by a nice cheerful man called Frank Turley: https://mplaza.training.

Even if you don't decide to use PRINCE2, if I had to pick out a few key points of it that will help you turn around your IT project, and then keep the project successful, I'd say it comes down to this:

- **Continued business justification**: know your business case, keep checking it makes sense, and keep monitoring progress against the business case, to get early warning of problems.

- **Defined roles and responsibilities**: know all the things that need to be done in order for the project to succeed, and know exactly who is responsible for doing them.

- **Highlight Report**: A report that gets sent to the senior people on the project, perhaps every week or every two weeks, detailing progress and raising any potential problems.

- **Project assurance**: this is a role undertaken by someone who isn't necessarily involved in your project on a day-to-day basis, but who is experienced in delivering successful IT projects, and can advise in order to help ensure that the project runs smoothly.

That's just scratching the surface, but I hope you can see the potential for how PRINCE2 could help you. It's well worth taking a look at it.

The official PRINCE2 manual is called *Managing Successful Projects with PRINCE2*, and the 2017 edition is the latest (as I write this in 2020). You can buy it from Amazon or the book store of your choice.

I'd recommend that you take a look at the various documents that PRINCE2 defines for projects, which gives you a handy checklist of things to think about when deciding how to monitor your project You'll find these in Appendix A of the PRINCE2 manual.

Activity 4.1: Identify people with project management and project assurance knowledge

It would be useful if at least one person in your project team understood PRINCE2. Doing the exams is best, but just listening to the audio course is a good start. Do you have anyone that could do this?

Without a shadow of a doubt, it will greatly increase your chances of success if you have someone outside of the day-to-day project team who can provide project assurance: a person who knows what good software development practices and project management practices look like, and can make sure they are followed. This should be someone with good experience, who has been involved in the successful delivery of previous projects, either inside or outside of your company. They can act as a coach or mentor to you, and also to the project team where required, to keep you on track. This is something you will need for the entire development period of your project, and quite likely for the operational lifetime of the software too, if you intend to continue developing and updating the software. Consistent monitoring and guidance is a key element of success, so don't overlook this.

PMP or APMP skills

PMP is the Project Management Professional qualification from the Project Management Institute (PMI). APMP is a similar qualification offered by the Association of Project Management. They are quite similar in some regards, although the PMP is more well-known in the USA, and APMP is more well-known in the UK and Europe. However, they both present a high quality body of knowledge of everything that is known about successful project management. The Project Management Body of Knowledge (PMBOK) published by the PMI for their PMP course contains a wealth of information, but it isn't the most accessible of documents, so a training course can help here.

A lot of people think that PRINCE2 competes with PMP (or APMP), but actually it doesn't: they work *together*. The PRINCE2 manual says that PMP is complementary to PRINCE2, and PMP repays the favour by saying that PRINCE is complementary to PMP. Here's why: Although PRINCE2 tells you *what* to do, it deliberately doesn't give you the techniques for *how* to do it, because there are a lot of potential techniques, and it would just make PRINCE2 far too big. So PRINCE2 will tell you that you need to do estimating, but it won't tell you how to do estimating. That's where PMP or APMP come in, to give you those additional skills and techniques. The body of knowledge that PMP or APMP covers is actually quite vast, and gives a good grounding in the skills needed for project management success on any type of project.

Personally, I don't think that PMP or APMP skills are quite as vital as PRINCE2 skills to IT projects, and I've certainly worked on a lot of successful IT projects that haven't formally relied on these skills, but they can be useful, especially on larger projects. It's definitely better to have these skills on the team than not to have them, but I'd say it's more of a nice-to-have than an essential component of success, based on my own experience.

Agile Development

What is agile?

Agile is a buzzword that you've probably heard, simply because everyone claims to be doing agile these days. (They're mostly not *actually* doing it, but the marketing people make them say they are!)

Agile on its own is a hugely broad term, and to be honest it is pretty meaningless in a lot of ways, unless you get more information. It's like someone telling you that they "play sport". Do they mean football, tennis or basketball? They all use a ball, but they are all very different games, with different skills and techniques involved.

It's actually easiest to define agile by telling you what it's not. It's very useful to understand this, so let me explain. Agile is *not* is the old-school method of software development, which is called waterfall. Waterfall is still used on many safety-critical projects, such as nuclear power stations or electronics for aircraft and spacecraft, but for most commercial software the waterfall approach doesn't work very well.

So what is waterfall, and why does it fail? Quite simply, waterfall development is a series of steps that you complete, and when you've done a step you don't go back to it. It's like water falling onto a series of lower and lower rocks: it can't flow back upstream.

Broadly speaking, the first step in waterfall is to gather *all* the requirements for the whole project, and write them up. Then you use these requirements to write a *full* specification of the whole system, which usually fits into several wheelbarrows. Then you wheel this specification to the developers, who spend a couple of years building everything exactly to the specification. Then, finally, the software is delivered to the customer… who rejects it as being not fit for purpose! Then the fun begins!

Why would the software not be fit for purpose? Lots of reasons, but here are three that are very easy to see and to understand:

- **Changing commercial environment**: Quite a lot can change in two years, and the commercial environment you were in back then is not the commercial environment you are in now. Competitors come and go, and customer expectations change.

- **Lack of user involvement**: Users don't get to try the software until it's finished, and then they realise that it doesn't meet their needs, after it has been fully developed and tested. That's when things are most expensive – and most difficult – to change.

- **Things get missed**: No matter how thorough the requirements and specification, things will be missed. That's human nature. It is almost impossible to write a totally complete and unambiguous set of requirements and specification, and to think of everything in advance. I have personally learned this the hard way, and so has almost everyone in the IT industry! To actually achieve perfection – which is what the waterfall methodology needs to be successful – you would need a huge amount of time, and a huge budget. For any project that you are likely to be involved in, perfection is just not going to happen, and you need to accept that all your documents will be in some way incomplete (although that's not an excuse not to aim high!)

So if agile isn't waterfall, what actually *is* agile? It's really just the exact opposite of waterfall. Agile, from our perspective here, is a series of techniques for software development that allow you to break down the project and work on it a little piece at a time, in a collaborative way. *The key idea is to get fast feedback from users and customers, and to respond rapidly to change.*

Although it varies a great deal from one project to the next, a typical agile project would look to do a new release of the software every 1 to 3 weeks, adding little pieces at a time, a new feature here and there, and incorporating comments from users and customers to guide development. It allows the business owner to specify priorities at short notice, every 1 to 3 weeks deciding what to work on next, reacting to the commercial environment. It also means you can't go too far off course, because you can see and track progress *in terms of delivered software* – things you can touch and feel even if you have no technical skill at all.

You might think that this sounds like unstructured chaos, but on a good project it's anything but.

The main agile approaches: Scrum and Kanban

Agile development is actually now quite a large branch of theory within software development and project management, and has fragmented into lots of different areas.

Within the broad umbrella of agile, the two dominant techniques you can choose between are called Scrum and Kanban. Most people think of Scrum when they think of agile. I won't go into too much depth on this, but Scrum essentially chooses a definite period of time, such as two weeks, calls this a Sprint, and sees how much work will fit into it. By contrast, Kanban has its origins in Japanese manufacturing and is more concerned with the flow of work through the system, and talks about visualising the work in progress and limiting the amount of work in progress—often interpreted in practice as working on one feature at a time and releasing it when it's ready. Kanban is used for software creation, and is also particularly well suited to support and maintenance activities which do not lend themselves to being time-boxed.

It depends on what you're trying to do as to which method is most effective. I've found that Scrum is hardest to bring into an organisation because the whole hierarchy of your company and your working methods have to change to support it. By contrast, Kanban doesn't change your processes to start with: you visualise progress, see problems, then transition to fix the problems. Both approaches benefit from cross-functional teams, where a group of people from across the company with different skills and expertise all come together—this usually includes software specialists and business specialists—and people at different levels in the organisational hierarchy.

Personally I've found Kanban often produces better results, so I'd recommend looking at that first. However, I've only scratched the surface of agile here, just to give you the basics. If you want to explore it further at some point, the Wikipedia article on <u>Agile Software Development</u> is actually a good place to start.

Getting results from agile

Most modern projects in commercial IT work on some form of agile, whether they know it or not, and it's an approach that I've personally used to great effect. I'd certainly recommend that you use some form of agile on your project (with a few exceptions, which are unlikely to apply to you). However, it's not a silver bullet, although it's sometimes presented as one. *Good people doing waterfall will do better than bad people doing agile.* Good waterfall projects continue to take place, as do bad agile projects! Ultimately, there's always going to be some level of requirements gathering, specification, development, testing, etc., taking place in every agile project—it just tends to happen very quickly, within the space of a week or two, like a mini-waterfall repeating over and over again.

Remember to focus on the results, not the methodology itself: a lot of today's agile zealots seem to put too much emphasis on the process, not on the results. Results, results, results!

There are a few more points of agile I want to pick up on, before we look at the Holy Texts of agile.

A key point of agile is to achieve **Validated Learning**, meaning that we learn as we go along, we learn early and often, and we learn mostly about what the customer wants and how we can satisfy their needs. This means favouring customer discovery over static prediction about what we think the customer might like.

Simplicity is also favoured by agile, defined neatly as "The art of maximizing the amount of work not done". This includes creating a **Minimum Viable Product (MVP)**, which is the smallest thing you could create in order to test an idea, get customer feedback, or get the project started with some tangible results.

Other, newer ideas linked to agile include **Continuous Delivery** and **Continuous Deployment**, where the process of testing software and pushing it out of the door to customers is largely automated, so that new features and fixes can be quickly and reliably made available to customers. This takes quite a lot of work to set up, but can pay dividends on larger projects, since it reduces the amount of manual work required when new software goes live.

Certifications

There are a few certifications in agile techniques, but none of these are particularly widely recognised, and there's no qualification that's become an industry-standard. Also, once you get going, agile working is mostly pretty simple and straightforward, unless you want to get fancy with it, so a bit of guidance is really all you need to get you on your way.

Just like PMP and APMP happily co-exist with PRINCE2, agile also sits nicely within PRINCE2, as the official PRINCE2 manual notes. Agile and PRINCE2 work together, they do not compete. There is actually now a certification called **PRINCE2 Agile**, offered by Axelos, the official PRINCE2 body, that brings both disciplines together.

Agile has inspired further lean techniques

From the early 2000s, agile spawned a renewed interest in similar **Lean** techniques, and many people became re-inspired by lean manufacturing, with techniques such as the Toyota Production System being adapted for use within software creation. Business people also became inspired by this, and created the "Lean Startup" movement. Authors such as Eric Ries with his book *The Lean Startup*, and Steve Blank with *The Startup Owner's Manual*, have a lot to say on this subject from a business point of view. Although this whole movement seems to have acquired the "startup" tag, I can assure you that these techniques apply far beyond startups, and are very useful in all manner of projects, especially ones where customer behaviour needs to be understood. I personally know of FTSE 100 companies—some of the largest companies in the world—who are using these approaches right now.

Activity 4.2: See if agile principles could help you

Back in 2001, a group of software developers got together and published 12 **Agile Principles**. These aim to show what an agile project requires; they also do a neat job of summarising the benefits that agile is likely to give you. They are now tested and proven on thousands of projects.

For this activity, simply read the 12 agile principles on the next page, think about how you could incorporate them into your project, and tick the ones you think would be useful to you. I suspect that you'll tick most of them, if not all of them.

Agile Principles

1. Customer satisfaction by rapid delivery of useful software.

2. Welcome changing requirements, even late in development.

3. Working software is delivered frequently (weeks rather than months).

4. Working software is the principal measure of progress.

5. Sustainable development, able to maintain a constant pace.

6. Close, daily cooperation between business people and developers.

7. Face-to-face conversation is the best form of communication (co-location).

8. Projects are built around motivated individuals, who should be trusted.

9. Continuous attention to technical excellence and good design.

10. Simplicity — the art of maximizing the amount of work not done — is essential.

11. Self-organizing teams.

12. Regular adaptation to changing circumstances.

Activity 4.3: See if the Agile Manifesto could help you

The **Agile Manifesto** is a very well-known summary of the ways in which agile projects work. It's the Gettysburg Address of agile software, really. It's incredibly short. Here it is:

Agile Manifesto

We are uncovering better ways of developing
software by doing it and helping others do it.

Through this work we have come to value:

Individuals and interactions over processes and tools
Working software over comprehensive documentation
Customer collaboration over contract negotiation
Responding to change over following a plan

That is, while there is value in the items on the
right, we value the items on the left more.

Let me interpret the agile manifesto for you, to put a bit more flesh on the bones, as they say.

It's saying that although processes and tools are useful, it's actually better to just speak to people, sit with people, work closely with people, and pool everyone's knowledge collaboratively. This implies that people are sitting together, which certainly helps, but isn't essential: for example, I successfully work with clients all over the world using Skype.

It's saying that we prefer not to have reams and reams of documentation, but some documentation is still useful, so that people know what they are supposed to be doing and aiming for. But rather than writing all the documentation up-front, in the form of huge requirements documents, it often fits the way that humans think and act to write less, spend more time on producing the software, and then correcting course as necessary. Working software allows you to see what's good, what's bad, and what needs to be changed, far more easily than documents do.

It's saying that although contracts are useful to cover yourself, in practice you get better results when developers and customers work together, rather than threatening legal action on each other! I've found that very often contracts can be breached but are never legally enforced, because it would irreparably damage a working relationship that needs to be kept intact. If things go bad, and a vendor threatens to completely pull out and leave you high and dry, you could sue them, and that might motivate some people, but suing will take forever while your business goes down the pan! So it's better to build a good collaborative working relationship from the start, nurture it, and take great care to see that a contract never has to be legally enforced in the first place (even though the contract will still be there to cover you if absolutely necessary).

Finally, it's saying that although a plan is a good and worthwhile thing to have, in the real world plans change, because market conditions change, and we need to respond to that.

So in this activity, I want you to consider if your project is sounding like it's governed by the things on the right hand side, and consider if you think that the things on the left hand side might help you. If you do, see if you can find ways to bring those techniques into your project.

Conclusion: What we achieved in step 4

I've given you a very brief outline of three very useful and co-existing sets of techniques: PRINCE2, complemented by PMP or APMP skills, and rounded out by agile development. I hope you've started to see, in a general sense, how PRINCE2 and agile, especially, can help you to get your project back on track.

This has all been grounding to prepare you for step 5, where we'll consider how to fix the specific problems that you identified your project as from suffering from at step 3. You can now see all these problems in the light of good project management practice and techniques.

How to fix your management problems

The last three steps are the real meat of turning your project around. ("Finally!", I can hear you crying! Sorry, but I had to give you a grounding in the basics first, or you'd miss the point of the rest of the steps.)

These steps represent a distilling of 20 years of my own personal experience, plus another 60 years of experience of the IT industry as a whole.

You don't need to read everything in this step if you're short on time: you can refer back to step 3 where you chose the root causes that you think apply to your project, and just home in on those root causes.

Without knowing your particular project and circumstances I can't tailor the advice specifically to you, so I'm going to take each root cause of failure in turn, and give some guidance and action steps that you can take to turn things around if you think that this root cause applies to your project. Of course, we have already dealt with poor project management in step 4, so I won't discuss that here.

The project is trying to achieve too much (scope is too wide)

"Doctor, it hurts when I do this".
"Well, stop doing it then!"
— *Tommy Cooper, comedian.*

If you're trying to do too much, and it's not working out, then do fewer things, but do them better! As an analogy, would you rather have 1 pound of the finest, best chocolate that the world has ever seen, or would you rather have 10 pounds of disgusting, sickening, cloying, greasy chocolate that gives you nausea every time you try to eat it?

Quality beats quantity!

Compromise on most other things before you compromise on quality. Often that means reducing the scope of work that you're trying to accomplish. We've discussed this earlier, so I won't labour the point. But a terrible system that's completely full of bugs won't usually achieve much of anything special. I'd rather have a system that does less, but actually does it properly.

Action points

Take your project breakdown diagram from Activity 2.1 and see if there are things you don't need to do at all, things you can do later in phase 2, 3, 4, etc, or things that might go away completely and not be necessary if you can put them off for long enough.

Be ruthless in your first draft of what you should cut, and then go back on it only if you can't bear to be without certain features. 80% of the benefit will come from 20% of the features, so don't be afraid to cut things out. Any gold-plating should be removed if you're struggling—you can add bells and whistles later after you start to be successful. Just aim to get something basic up and running, and the momentum from that will carry you to success.

Unrealistic expectations

A common disappointment with software projects is that the resulting software isn't perfect, and sometimes there are problems. Let me tell you now: *every software project will have bugs and defects in it*. Even the software used in airliners has been proven, in study after study, to contain multiple defects. Terrifying but true!

Don't expect perfection, because you won't get it. (At least not until you run out of time, money, and sanity!)

I'm not saying to settle for mediocrity here: the skill is in knowing what to accept, what not to accept, and putting in place a system to deal with problems and defects (which we'll look at in the section "Poor reporting and handling of bugs and defects" in step 6). A lot of this comes from experience, which is why having someone with good software development knowledge, to act as *project assurance*, is important.

Another unrealistic expectation is trying to get things done in too short a time span. I have had software development clients who say, "Do this, and make it really good, but don't spend too much time on it!" Hmmm, not sure how to do that one, boss! It's going to take as long as it's going to take, unless you tell me I can drop the quality requirements to get it done rough-and-ready. Remember the trade-offs between time, cost, quality and scope that we discussed earlier?

Don't let your development team get away with murder, but equally you've got to give them time to do what they need to do. This comes down to two things: having a good team that you can trust, and having someone experienced in software development and successful IT projects to keep an eye on things, to know what is reasonable and what is not. (It's project assurance again.)

Action points

Look at the bad things in your project—defects, uncompleted work—and decide whether your expectations might be too high. Are you asking for a rocket ship to Mars to be ready by next week?

If you're not sure whether your expectations are realistic or not, talk to somebody with more experience of delivering software projects.

If your expectations *are* realistic, and aren't being met, then we'll look elsewhere in this step at what you can do about it.

If your expectations aren't realistic, then work with your team to understand where they think you are asking for too much, and see where you can compromise. (In this instance, compromise isn't a dirty word.)

Unarticulated project goals

If your project isn't meeting its goals, do people actually know what the goals are?

This goes back to our earlier work on project benefits. One of the reasons I got you to list the measurable benefits that your project is seeking to achieve is so that you can clearly communicate these expected benefits to everyone on the team. This will keep them focused on what you *actually* want, not what they *think* you want. You've got to give your team the big picture, so they can base the decisions they take on making sure they meet your overall objectives.

Action points

Make sure you've done the activity to list the measurable benefits for your project. Get your project goals clear.

Then communicate your goals to everyone in the team. Even if you *think* they should all know what the benefits and goals are, there might well be confusion, so communicate again, and communicate clearly. A single page, or preferably just a few lines or bullet points, is all it takes. Issue this by email, then print it out in big letters and stick it on the wall.

Wrong people on the project

Good people can overcome a lot of problems. Bad people will cause a lot of problems.

People are so important to the success of your project that I'll skip discussion of it here, and devote the entirety of step 7 to talking about people.

Marketing failure

I've seen a lot of IT projects that have delivered good software, but have failed because customers didn't like it, or customers didn't buy it. In short, customers didn't see the value, and they didn't feel the benefits.

When I say "marketing" here, I'm thinking about several things:

1. Marketing communications, for example your advertising messages and slogans.
2. Your sales team and sales process.
3. Your market segmentation, targeting, positioning and pricing: how you go to market.
4. How your project fits into the wider context of your business: how your project and your other business activities help to push each other forward (key buzzword: synergy).

Marketing is a huge topic, and although I study, practice, and am qualified to advise on it I will not do so here, since it would take too long to do justice to the topic for you.

Make sure you fully understand the marketing for your project, as I have defined it above. If you need to brush up your marketing, a very good and practical book that gets results is *No B.S. Direct Marketing (third edition)* by Dan Kennedy.

Action points

A lot of the action points here might seem basic, but please don't overlook them. They are the foundations of marketing success. Consider these action points as a very brief collection of ideas to jog your memory.

Ask yourself this: are you actually building something that customers can see the value in? If not, step back, refocus your project, consider focus groups and other forms of user testing and user feedback, and consider changing what you are building. I've had some very powerful results from running some focus groups, which isn't as scary as it sounds! A very good book on how to get results from focus groups is *Focus Groups: A Practical Guide for Applied Research* by Richard A. Krueger and Mary Anne Casey.

Are you positioning yourself to communicate the value of the software clearly to the customer, in language that the customer can understand? The classic book on positioning is *Positioning: The battle for your mind*, by Ries and Trout.

Do you have a clear Unique Selling Proposition (USP)? I feel almost guilty saying this, because it's such a cliché, below the level of even marketing 101, but really, you need to check it.

Are you selling to the right customers? Define your ideal customer in as much detail as you can, so that you can focus your marketing firepower on them. This is an easy area to skip or overlook, but the better you know your customers for this particular project the better the project will be.

Do you have a clear marketing plan and marketing calendar, spelling out how you will reach your customers, and detailing your message, market, and media?

Consider whether you need to adjust your project budget, to spend less on software development and more on sales and marketing.

Do you need to call in additional help in Search Engine Optimization (SEO), Pay Per Click advertising (PPC), Public Relations (PR) or other disciplines to help spread the word?

What user insights can you glean from Google Analytics, if you are running a website or web project?

(Note that SEO, analytics, and other online marketing disciplines are now so advanced and niched that nobody can possibly be an expert in everything, so you might need to call in the specialists to give you a short-term skills boost in these areas.)

Inadequate support from leaders and upper management

If people don't think your project is important, they won't treat it as important. They won't give your their best work.

If people think that the project will get canned or killed, or it's just another initiative that will fizzle out, then you have no power to demand or expect success.

Fortunately there's not much else to say about this topic! Just get your top people enthusiastic.

Action points

Support your project. Talk about it. Explain the benefits to the company. Explain the benefits to the individuals that work on the project. Explain that you are firmly behind the project. Mention the project frequently. Keep energy and enthusiasm up. Keep a positive mental attitude even when things are looking bleak.

Focus on benefits and results. Get other senior leaders to do the same. Email the project goals to your team, and put them on the wall in large letters, to prove your commitment.

Ask for a regular Highlight Report (to use PRINCE2 language) to track progress and to *show that you care about the project*.

Poor reporting of the project's status

If senior management can't keep track of what is going on, the project will go off track. It's as simple as that. People have their own ideas about what should happen, and they might not match *your* ideas!

Once you've clearly communicated the measurable benefits and goals of your project, to set expectations, you need to follow up to make sure that the benefits are being attained and the goals are being met.

Agile development, where working software is built and delivered gradually, one piece at a time, is great for tracking progress: either something is done and released, or it is not done. You can't have the wool pulled over your eyes with this: if it can't be demonstrated as working, then it's not working, and it's not done! With this technique you need zero technical knowledge to check up on whether something has been done.

However, the project is wider than just tracking the results as they come in. You need to know about the risks you face, your priorities for development, quality problems, etc.

This is where the Highlight Report from PRINCE2 comes in useful. It provides a nice format to make sure you stay on top of things as a senior manager. The full explanation of a Highlight Report is in the Appendix of the PRINCE2 manual, but it focusses on reporting the work in progress and the work to be done next, what has been completed, corrective actions required, how the project is performing against the tolerances for time and cost, change requests, key issues and risks, and any lessons learned along the way.

A regular Highlight Report is really about accountability: holding yourself and others to account. Many leaders and entrepreneurs find that working with a coach or a mastermind group helps them to achieve more because they are being held accountable for success, with the coach or other group members following up to make sure that progress has been achieved.

Action points

Even if you are involved in the project quite closely, you need the discipline of a clear, written Highlight Report, produced at regular intervals (every week, every two weeks, every month, or whatever suits you). It focusses the mind of everyone on the project, getting them to think about results, and keeping you informed.

You should also ask for regular demonstrations of new features, to track progress with your own eyes.

Inaccurate estimates of needed resources

Estimates in software development are very hard to get right. You will read articles about people who claim to have discovered some kind of deep truth about how to produce accurate estimates. You will also read articles about Elvis being alive and living on the moon. I have as much faith in one of these types of articles being correct as the other.

People have developed all kinds of weird, wacky and overly-elaborate methods for estimating how long it will take to complete some software development task. I won't bore you with them.

So why is estimating so hard in software development? A lot of people have thought about this problem, but here's my take on it: quite simply, estimating is hard because you are always doing work that hasn't been done before, at least not in the same way, not on the same project, and not with the same people. Plus, you're never usually working on just one thing at a time, and you get pulled into meetings and other things that consume your time and distort your perception. So you never build up a good store of knowledge from which to make a good estimate.

If you are building a bridge across a river, bridges have been built lots of times before, in pretty much the same way, and there is a good body of knowledge as to what needs to be done, in what order, and how long it takes. You can also physically see progress of the bridge as it is built. By contrast, it's harder to touch and feel software, and harder to see progress. That's why good progress reports, and regular demonstrations of software features, are useful.

Also, bear in mind that *a good software developer is at least 10 times as productive as an average software developer*. Studies have shown this (I'll discuss it more in step 7), my own experience has shown this to me, and I probably understate the case. Unless you know exactly who will be working on something, you can't accurately estimate it either, for just this reason.

Software development is one of those things where you often only find all the hurdles and problems when you actually get down to the details of doing it. You might find that there's a problem in a web browser, or a problem with some third-party software you're using, or that doing something will break something else in the software, and that suddenly consumes a lot of time to fix it. This will throw your estimates off.

You'll notice I've only talked about the estimating of *time* here, not about the estimating of *cost*. Time is money, and costs on a software project are largely a matter of time taken. (I'll deal in step 7 with the issue of hiring cheap developers, who take more time, still do a worse job, and thus give a false economy.)

Beware of amateurs who have just a little knowledge of professional development, who say, "I could write this software myself in a couple of days, so why will it take you two weeks?" There is a wide gap between software that's been quickly hacked to work for the time being, and software that's been properly written to be testable, supportable, and maintainable for the long-term!

Action points

The best way I've found to estimate the time a software development task will take is to ask everyone involved how long they think something will take, get them to explain their reasons in order to figure out any problems that other people might not have foreseen, and then either build a consensus or just take an average of these estimates. In the Scrum agile methodology there is a technique called Planning Poker, which is similar to this. The power and benefit of this technique is that it pools the knowledge of the whole team, in case anybody can think of a problem or issue that will slow down or speed up development. On a software project, different people bring very different knowledge and skills to the project, and some will know various parts of the system better than others, so it's good to get people together for estimating. Also, good communication like this will sometimes share enough knowledge to prevent people from making a change that would damage another area of the system.

Keep a track of your estimates, and compare them to finished results. If you consistently over-estimate or under-estimate, take that into account when producing future estimates.

If estimating is a big problem for you, study PMP or APMP, which deal with estimating techniques in more detail.

Risk and unforeseen circumstances play a large part in making estimates inaccurate. It's usually best to attempt the most risky pieces of a problem first, and reduce the uncertainty as quickly as you can, which will improve future estimates for time and cost.

Stakeholder politics and lack of stakeholder consent

This is more a subject for Machiavelli than it is for me! Personally I'm not one for playing politics: I pretty much tell the truth as I see it, and you either like it or you don't! (You *should* like it though, because presenting the truth in an accurate, positive and helpful way will get us to success more quickly.)

The term *stakeholder* refers to anyone with any kind of interest in your project. There's very little I can say about stakeholder politics, other than to try and resolve problems as early in the project as you can, and not to put them off in the hope that they go away. You need the whole team to be pulling in the same direction, and that requires clear leadership. If they're not, consider removing people from the team.

Lack of stakeholder consent is an interesting problem to consider, and it's often overlooked. If your project is to automate a process, which will then make people redundant, they just might not give you the full extent of their knowledge and cooperation in developing the automated process! I have seen this happen surprisingly often, so be alert for it.

I'll keep this section short, but it's surprising how the motivations and desires of various project stakeholders might not be the same as yours, so give stakeholder politics some thought and don't overlook it. Is there someone connected with your project that might not be going all-out for success?

Action points

The techniques taught in PRINCE2, PMP and APMP for risk assessment, risk management and stakeholder management are very useful here, since stakeholder politics and lack of stakeholder consent are really about assessing risk and putting measures in place to cope with that.

Leadership skills, again touched upon on PMP and APMP, are also required. Don't be afraid to pull rank and lay down the law if it means getting the project back on track. You're the boss!

Commercial pressures

Here's a few examples of commercial pressures:

- "We have to release this feature now because Competitor X has it, and we don't want to be left behind."
- "This feature must be released by 1st May, whether it's ready or not!"
- "We're going to have to cut the project budget by 50%. We still need you to deliver everything though."

These might sound fairly reasonable to a business person, and at the end of the day it's the business that should drive the software, not the other way round. But the reason commercial pressures like these can cause projects to fail is largely because they affect the *quality* of the product that can be delivered.

Action points

Check that your "commercial pressures" actually are as important as you think they are.

Are your commercial pressures enough to put the entire project in jeopardy? If so, go back to basics—step 1 of this book— and consider whether the measurable benefits of your project are still desirable and achievable.

Consider the trade-off between time, cost, quality, scope, and benefits. Do you need to increase the budget or decrease your quality requirements now?

Try hard not to sacrifice quality, at least not below the level that you would deem acceptable. It's nearly always best to cut scope rather than quality—do less, but do it well.

Built the wrong thing to solve the business problem

Maybe your software is perfect, but it's just not getting the business benefits you expected of it. If it's not a marketing problem, then perhaps you built the wrong thing, or tackled the problem in the wrong way.

For example, if your aim was to reduce calls to the call centre by 50% by investing in a better self-service help system, and actually you've only reduced calls by 10%, maybe the self-service help system wasn't the right way to go, or maybe you need to do something else as well in order to meet your goal. Perhaps that could be providing better user guides with the initial product, making the product itself easier to use, providing more pre-sales support, selling to more sophisticated customers, etc. We'll look at this in more detail below, in the section "Poor user training and documentation".

Notice that some of these solutions are technical, and some are not.

Action points

Identify whether you might have built the wrong thing. If the quality of your software is good, but you're not getting the expected results, you've probably missed something and built the wrong thing, or not built enough. This is one of the rare cases where you might need to *increase* the scope of your project.

Review early, and review often, whether your project is on track to deliver the benefits required. You can do this with a Highlight Report, and by closely tracking the benefits received. The earlier you catch problems, the earlier you can consider changing what your project is delivering, to make sure it delivers the benefits.

Consider some small-scale, rapid experiments that you could use to test whether an alternative solution could deliver the benefits better than what you are currently doing. Remember the 80-20 rule: if 80% of benefits come from 20% of the software, consider building some portion of that 20% quickly, and testing it, to see if it leads you down a better path to getting more benefits, faster.

Poor user training and documentation

Sometimes the software is right, and it's solving the right problem in the right way, but you're not getting results because people just don't know how to use it. This usually comes down to inadequate training, and/or inadequate documentation.

User training and documentation should be thought of very early in the development of the software (although, sadly, usually they are left as an afterthought). This is because good user training takes time and money, and both need to be budgeted.

Another benefit of considering user training early is that it forces you to confront exactly who your users are and what level of training they will need in order to use the software effectively. Are the users highly technically skilled, or are they novice computer users? Have they used similar software before, or is this a brand new experience for them? Are they migrating from a different system – computer-based or paper-based – with ingrained habits? Know your users well, and you'll know how to help them get the best out of your software.

If you can identify that training will be a specific problem, this is sometimes an early warning sign that you need to simplify the software. Even if you don't decide to simplify, you can build better features into the software to guide the user as they go along. This can include help pop-ups that appear the first time a user sees a particular screen, and on-screen help text that appears all the time to guide the user. Your goal should be that the software is straight-forward and self-explanatory, so that the users don't have to refer to the help or documentation often, and do not require lengthy training. The perfect scenario is to make the software so intuitive that people never need to consult the formal documentation.

Modern help for software can take lots of different formats. I'll cover a few of those now.

You can use a helpdesk-style Knowledge Base tool, such as **Zendesk**, which works by letting you publish lots of little articles. See http://www.zendesk.com.

If you have trouble keeping your documentation up to date (and most people do), you could use one of my favourite tools, a wiki, which lets users update the documentation themselves as they go along. This is just like Wikipedia, where anyone (that you have granted permission to) can update the documentation. This works very well in practice, and I'm a big fan of using a wiki to document your software. It works because it's easier to make small changes to the documentation at the exact point that you realise they are required, rather than having some huge formal process to update all the documentation at once. It also helps with pooling knowledge and letting users share with each other how to get the best results out of the software. There are lots of wiki providers, but personally I've had a lot of success with **Atlassian Confluence**. See https://www.atlassian.com/software/confluence.

I've found that quite often, a short help video that guides the user is very useful for training. For initial training you can make the videos quite long, perhaps 20-30 minutes each, but for quick help while the user is actually using the application, it's good to split the videos up into short task-focussed videos, so rather than having a single video that's one hour long and covers lots of things, you'd have a short two minute video on how to set up a new user, and another short video on how to run a sales report, etc. These videos where you can see the screen, with a user talking and moving the mouse to show what to do, are called *screencasts*. You can use either Camtasia (PC or Mac) or Screenflow (Mac only) for making screencasts.

Moving away from the help itself, there are other things you can do to improve the usability of your software. Better error messages can often help to guide the user. Writing good error messages is an art-form all to itself. A good error message should be written in clear English, should explain what has gone wrong, what the consequences of this error are, and should explain what the user should do next to fix it. A bad error message, that leaves the user floundering, would say something like, "An error occurred." A good error message would say something like, "There is no paper in the printer, so your document could not be printed. Please load paper into Tray 1 and click the Print button again."

Action points

First, decide how skilled you think your users currently are in using your software. Give them an average grading out of 10. Next, decide how skilled they need to be in order to get the business benefits from the software. This gives you an idea of the sort of gap we're going to need to close here. Then you can decide on which methods are most appropriate.

Decide whether you think a helpdesk knowledge base, a wiki, and/or some tutorial videos are required. Decide on whether face-to-face training is required, and who should give it. If you don't know where to start, I'd recommend a wiki because it's quickest to do, then some screencast videos. (Videos can sometimes take a surprisingly long time to make.)

Allow anyone to contribute, encourage people to update the wiki whenever they learn something new or the software changes, and soon you will have a good guide to the system, that's not outdated, and that people can learn from. This is also useful for Continuous Improvement, which may be of interest to you if your company is ISO:9001 certified.

Try to avoid keeping the knowledge in people's heads: you don't want people to leave your company and take all the knowledge with them: it's better to have as much as you can written down and documented for everybody to benefit from.

Failure to proactively manage risk

Many projects get derailed by unforeseen events. With a bit of discipline though, you can actually foresee lots of events that might cause problems, and plan in advance how to deal with them. Fortunately for us, it's fairly easy to do.

PRINCE2 has an excellent discussion of risk; it's chapter 8 in the PRINCE2 manual. It's pretty much the last word in risk management as far as most projects are concerned (including your project, most likely). I won't repeat that discussion here, because it's quite detailed, but it will be time very well spent if you read it, and I really hope that you do. I'll also base this section of the book largely on PRINCE2: their approach is well-documented and proven to be effective, which sounds like a winner to me!

Let me just give you an executive summary of what we're trying to achieve when we look at risk. The chapter opens by summing it up nicely, saying: "Management of risk should be systematic and not based on chance. It is about the proactive identification, assessment and control of risks that might affect the delivery of the project's objectives... The aim is to support better decision making through a good understanding of risks – their causes, likelihood, impact, timing, and the choice of responses to them."

If your project is especially risky, you might find a specialist course in risk management useful, such as the M_O_R (Management of Risk) certification. That's overkill for most of us, but you can find out more at https://www.axelos.com/best-practice-solutions/mor.

Some people think of risks only as bad things, or threats. However, some people, and PRINCE2, consider opportunities to also be a type of risk – think of it as a possible event that would have a good outcome rather than a bad outcome. An example of this would be the possibility that we only need one round of User Acceptance Testing, and not two rounds as we are currently planning. This would allow us to release the software to customers earlier. By identifying this, and managing it as a risk by planning a response, we could decide to hold a rehearsal of the testing to increase the probability of only needing one round of testing.

Although it's good to plan to maximise opportunities, to keep things simple here I'll just talk about threats: the things you want to avoid. They're the things that will really sink your project.

What risk management is all about

Let's get down to brass tacks here. What risk management is all about is figuring out everything that could go wrong, seeing how likely it would be to happen and how bad it would be if it did, then determining *before the bad event happens* what you are going to do about it. You can often take actions at the start of your project – or right where you are now – to make certain events less likely to happen, or to strengthen your ability to cope with them.

To say this another way:
Planning and Preparation Prevent Poor Performance.

PRINCE2 tells us that you're really looking to do five things when it comes to risk:

1. **Identify** the risks
2. **Assess** the risks to see how bad they are
3. **Plan** your responses that will keep the project on track
4. **Implement** your planned responses
5. **Communicate** what you're doing to everyone who needs to know

There are lots of techniques for risk management. I'll cover the single most common technique, which is useful in most cases, and then we'll look at some examples of the various responses that you can take to risk. If you've not seen these before, they should give you some idea of the level of control you can exert over risk, and master the unknown before it masters you!

How to track your risks: use a risk register

Risks change over the lifetime of your project: some come, some go, and some change their *likelihood* or *severity*. Risk management isn't something you just do once, it has to be an on-going task. To do this, you need what's often called a risk register, and you've probably seen one before, because they're quite common. The risk register is often done in Microsoft Excel, and it's just a table which lists, for each risk, at least these few things: Risk description, probability of it happening (before you do anything about it), impact if it happened, an overall risk value for how bad the risk is, and what your response is to that risk. (You can find a full description of headings for a risk register in the appendix of the PRINCE2 manual if you're interested.)

You can choose to record probability and severity in words, eg Low, Medium, High, or by using a number such as 1 to 5, where 1 is lowest and 5 is highest. I recommend using numbers for probability and severity, because then you can multiply them

Risk Description	Prob	Sev	Score (P x S)	Risk Response
Software might not be ready in time for the trade show	3	4	12	Transfer: The software development company's contract has been written so that they will pay compensation if the software is delayed.
The tax report generated by the system might be incorrect	2	4	8	Reduce: During testing we will ask a tax specialist to review the report.
Web server is unreachable due to network failure	1	2	2	Accept: Too expensive to install a standby server.

Figure 3. A simple risk register, showing the Probability, Severity, and Score, ordered with the highest Score first.

to give an overall score, to let you sort the risks and deal with the most severe risks first.

You can set a *risk threshold,* so that the low-scoring minor risks can be dealt with by the project manager, whereas the higher-scoring major risks are escalated to you as the senior manager, so that you can keep control over the major risks on the project.

When you include your *risk responses,* which we'll look at next, a simple risk register might look something like this:

Even in this short example you can see the benefit in identifying the risks early and up-front, using a proper technique, rather than just idle chatter. Because we properly understood that the software might not be ready in time for a trade show, and that this was a serious problem, we could negotiate the contract with the software developer to incentivise on-time delivery and penalise failure, which would recover some of our costs. We also realised that it would be a problem if the tax report was wrong – never cross the taxman! – so we recognised the need to arrange for a specialist to review this. We also decided that it wouldn't be worth having a standby server for our website, because the low probability and low severity of the server going down wasn't worth the high cost to set up and maintain a standby server.

How to respond to risks you have identified

The risk responses—the actions you can take once you have identified a risk—are very interesting and very valuable in terms of keeping your project on the right track to success. You might not have seen these before. Again, PRINCE2 gives us a very useful list of six risk responses, so we'll use that. Personally I think it's sometimes arguable as to whether a particular response falls under one category or another, and you could even argue about some of my examples below. However, that's one for the theorists, and it doesn't really matter to us in the real world: you just need to understand what your options are, so you can do something sensible to keep your project on track.

Here are the six main risk responses:

Avoid: Make a big change to your project so that the risk is no longer possible. For example, if your project was to provide software to users in a country with very poor internet access, a big risk would be a loss of internet connection. To avoid this risk you could choose to build software that runs entirely on a user's PC and never needs to access the internet.

Reduce: Take steps to reduce the probability of the bad event occurring, and/or to reduce the severity of it if it does happen. For example, consider the risk of employees who are new to your call centre not understanding how to use your call centre software. To reduce the probability of this happening, face-to-face training could be given, rather than just using a training manual. To reduce the severity of any new users arriving and not knowing how to use the system, you could arrange to pair-up new and experienced users, so the new user will have someone to answer their questions.

Fallback: Put in place a set of actions to be followed IF the bad event occurs. It's really a Plan B. For example, if you are making sure your website is available for customers during business hours, you could identify a risk that your main web server could go down, and the fallback action would be to switch to using a standby server in another data centre.

Transfer: Give some or all of the risk to a third-party. This can often mean insurance or a clause in a contract. For example, there is a risk that your software development company might not have a demo system ready for an important trade show. You could transfer this risk by putting a clause in the development company's contract that they would pay you damages in the event of a delay.

Accept: Deliberately do nothing, and just accept the risk. This is usually because it is more cost-effective than the alternatives. The risk should continue to be monitored though, because it could increase in probability or severity at some point. For example, to take a common real-world scenario, if you have identified a risk that your web server could go down due to network problems, but this isn't too likely, it wouldn't greatly inconvenience users if the site was down for an hour or two, and the cost of creating and supporting a standby server was high, you might just accept the risk that the website could be unavailable for some time. You need to monitor this type of risk response though, because if a very important customer suddenly starts using this system, the downtime might then become unacceptable and you could no longer accept the risk, so you would have to reduce it by adding a standby server.

Share: Share the pain or gain of an unknown event with a third party. This is often based on a contract or agreement. For example, you might agree with your software development company that if the software is late then they will give you a discount on any remaining time required until the software is delivered.

As I said above, it's debatable as to how exactly you would classify these risk responses, but you should just be aware of the different options you have when it comes to planning how to minimise your risks.

Action points

It's quite simple to make sure your project doesn't fail due to badly handled risks. I recommend starting by reading the chapter in the PRINCE2 manual which covers risk. Then set up a risk register—a list of risks and responses—like the example here (or if you want to be a bit more fancy then see the appendix of the PRINCE2 manual).

The real value is in thinking about all the risks you face, understanding how likely they are to prevent you from succeeding, and then deciding what you are going to do about each risk. Involve everyone in your team in identifying risks, because each person will have a different perspective and could well see things that you will miss.

Remember to regularly review your risk register, because risks, their probability and severity can all change over time.

Wrong decision to build software vs customizing an existing package

At the start of any IT project, you always make a fundamental decision: do we get some software built from scratch, or do we take an existing software package and customise it? This decision is often known as "buy versus build", and an existing software package is often referred to as Commercial Off-The-Shelf (COTS) software.

If your project is already underway, it might be too late to change your approach... or it might not be. It really comes down to whether or not you think there are so many problems with what you're doing now that it's worth starting again. This means evaluating your sunk costs, and this is an area where many people go wrong, so we'll look at it now.

The faulty logic is to say "Well, we've spent $300,000 on it so far, if we kill the project we'll have wasted that money." That $300,000 is gone. You can't get it back. It's a **sunk cost**. What you should really be asking is "How much additional money would it take to finish the project this way, versus changing our approach and starting again?" If it would take $100,000 to finish the job with the current approach, but only $50,000 to finish the job with a new approach, that's something you have to consider. Often people lack the confidence to make this kind of decision because they think it will make them look bad. It's often a political choice, rather than a financial choice, so make sure you've got the political firepower to back you up if you decide to change your approach!

Notice that even if you do decide to change your approach, throw away your existing solution and start again, you've still got things you can salvage, such as requirements, test data, a project team, probably some user and customer feedback, and crucially the learning and experience that you got from doing it the first time round.

Ask yourself: **"Has somebody already built something that can do what we need to do?"**

If the software is for something which is a common commodity, such as payroll processing, accounting, or word processing, you should almost certainly choose something off-the-shelf. By contrast, if the software will be your secret sauce—your *core competence* to use the jargon—then you will be more likely to build the software (or have it built specially for you) to give you an advantage over your competitors.

Build or buy?

So what are the things to consider when deciding whether to build a new software system or just buy in an existing system? At the highest level it's actually the same as when you're thinking about your project plan. You need to consider the six project variables from PRINCE2, plus "Resources" (mentioned in PMP):

- **Time**: What will get you the quickest results? Usually this is buying a package.
- **Cost**: What will be cheapest? Again, this is likely to be buying a package.
- **Quality**: What will give you the quality you require?
- **Scope**: Is there a package available that can do everything you want?
- **Benefits**: Will a package allow you to fully realise the business benefits of the project?
- **Risks**: What are the risks of each approach, buy versus build, on your particular project? We'll look at these below.
- **Resources**: Are the people in your organisation, or the people you can hire, more likely to be able to successfully deliver a solution based on buying or building?

Benefits of buying a COTS package and customizing it

There are lots of potential benefits to buying a software package and customizing it, if you do it right. You won't always get all of the benefits listed here, but if done properly, buying an existing package and customizing it can give you the following benefits:

- **Time**: Quicker than building it yourself, so faster for you to get to market, because the base product is usually ready to go almost as soon as you buy it.

- **Time**: You can quickly catch up with the industry leaders if you are using the same software as they are.

- **Time**: You can more quickly match and exceed the increasingly high expectations of customers.

- **Time**: Less management hassle than building it yourself, because you don't need to recruit developers and testers.

- **Cost**: Cheaper than building it yourself, because fewer staff and less time are required.

- **Quality**: More reliable than building it yourself because the software has been used and tested by lots of other companies (although this won't be true of your customizations to the underlying package).

- **Quality**: Easier to use, because there is better documentation and support from the vendor.

- **Quality**: Higher quality if there are multiple vendors in the market, because competition should drive up quality.

- **Quality**: More secure, because more customers have used the software and potentially found any security problems.

- **Quality**: Easier to keep up to date, because the vendor will be bringing out new versions of the software.

- **Quality**: You can benefit from the experience and best-practice of other companies, and the feedback that they have given the vendor, all of which might well have been baked into the software.

- **Scope**: More features, and probably more fully-fleshed-out features, because the software has been developed by dedicated industry specialists over a long period of time.

- **Time, cost, quality**: Ongoing maintenance is easier because this will be done by the vendor, and you don't have to worry about recruiting and retaining your own software developers and testers.

Drawbacks of buying a COTS package and customizing it

- **Cost**: You could get locked in to a certain vendor, who could increase prices.

- **Cost**: If you cannot easily find people to customise the package it could become expensive to make changes.

- **Cost**: Are you fully aware of all the costs? Are there any hidden charges now or later? Is the vendor aiming to price low to win the business then lock you in and put up prices?

- **Quality**: In some cases there might not be many packages to choose from, in an uncompetitive market, so quality might be low and prices might be high.

- **Quality**: The package might not do everything you want it to do, and might not be capable of ever doing some of those things.

- **Quality**: You are largely at the mercy of the vendor as to what features get supported and which don't, both now and in the future.

- **Quality**: You are less likely to formally test the software, and more likely to assume that it will just work, so you might not spot defects and problems (for example, how can you be sure that the financial reports that the software produces are in fact accurate?).

- **Quality**: Vendors must keep adding new features to be able to keep selling new versions of their product, and over time the software can get bloated, complicated and much harder to use (many people would cite Microsoft Office as an example of this).

- **Quality**: Even if you can change the software, the changes might be incomplete, made too slowly, or be insufficient to meet your needs.

- **Scope**: You are likely to have to change your business processes to fit the software, and not have the software adapt to your processes. This can sometimes be a *very* big problem: it affects people, morale, results, and often customers too. Do not underestimate this as a problem.

- **Scope**: If you are only using the same package as everyone else then how can you innovate to beat your competition?

- **Risk**: Will your data be secure if it is kept on the vendor's systems?

- **Risk**: Can you export the data to another system if you decide to change vendor?

- **Risk**: Will the people customizing the software break Non-Disclosure Agreements and reveal details of your business to their other customers (who could be your competitors).

- **Risk**: The vendor could go out of business or stop supporting the product, leaving you with difficulties in supporting, maintaining, and further developing the software, which could become obsolete.

What to look for when choosing a software package to buy

If you decide to go down the route of buying a Commercial Off-The-Shelf package and customizing it, then what should you look for in the package? Here are the main things:

- Are you looking for a piece of software in an area where almost everybody buys a solution, rather than building their own? This would include e-commerce and accountancy packages. The most obvious example is a word processor or spreadsheet: nobody would write their own, they'd just use Microsoft Office.

- Does the package do everything you want? This will mean making a list of your core requirements, which could be quite extensive, then your nice-to-have requirements.

- Is there a good choice of packages from different vendors? This is likely to mean a competitive market, where prices are better.

- How many other people are using the package? How many customers does the vendor have? There's often safety in numbers: the most popular packages are likely to be supported, maintained and improved. You ideally want a package with a good market share.

- How many people can provide customization services? A competitive market for this will keep prices down. By contrast, if only the vendor can customise the software it might become more expensive.

- How long has the software been on the market? Look for mature software that has been on the market for several years. This will have had time to become stable, and you won't be the guinea pig! Version 1.0 or 2.0 of any software will need particularly careful testing by you.

Benefits of building the software rather than buying it

To understand the benefits and drawbacks of building the software yourself, in a lot of cases you can just see these as the exact opposite of the benefits and drawbacks of buying and customizing COTS software packages, which we've discussed above. However, there are a few other things that are unique to building software, either doing it internally or by outsourcing, which I'll cover here.

The benefits of building software are:

- **Time**: You can be more responsive to change, because you aren't tied to a vendor's timescales and schedules (this usually applies only after the initial time taken to build the first version of the software).

- **Quality**: Your software can be unique, which can give you a competitive advantage.

- **Quality**: You can properly support your own business processes, which is useful if your processes are particularly good or innovative.

- **Quality**: Your employees and other people are likely to be particularly knowledgeable about your company, your industry and your customers, and this valuable knowledge can lead to a more suitable solution.

Action Points

Consider whether you need to radically change your approach, switching between buy and build. The further you are into the project then the tougher it will be to change, although that doesn't mean it's not the right answer. Even if you decide to totally change your approach, you will still have lessons and learning from the work you have already done, so you can do your best not to make the same mistakes again.

This choice of buy versus build is very dependent on your particular project. However, I can tell you that **most people these days tend to buy a package rather than building from scratch wherever possible**, and I think this can be the best approach for many companies.

Studies also point towards a higher chance of success when buying and customizing a COTS package than when building software, but it's such a situation-dependent area that what's true in a general study might or might not turn out to be true for you.

Sorry to sit on the fence there, but at least you now have a good understanding of the issues you will need to consider!

People are trying to do too many things at the same time

We've already talked about scope, which you can think of as being how many things your project is going to do. But the amount of things you try to do at once can also have a big bearing on whether you succeed.

Trying to do too many things at once is often linked to just trying to do too much overall. In other words, your project might be too ambitious (your scope is too big), or your deadline might be too tight (your schedule needs adjusting).

The problem with doing too many things at once is you always lack focus. By contrast, when you focus on one thing, you start to see it in more detail, and you have all that detail in your head. You can find the problems, the weird exceptional cases that you will have to deal with, and do a really thorough job. But when you start focusing on too many things at once, and being pulled all over the place, you can only do everything superficially. You miss the detail. You forget the important facts. You do a poor job.

Trying to do too much can be a problem that affects either an individual or the whole team. It can be a drawback of agile development, where a team typically works in an iterative style, coding one set of features whilst working on the requirements for what's coming next.

Back when I was working a summer job during my university years, I preferred it when my boss only gave me one or two things at a time to work on, rather than giving me huge stacks of work at a time. I found my brain wanted to jump between all the things at once, as the ideas came to me, rather than working on things in a disciplined manner. I still think that's true today, looking at all the things I'm working on in my own business and with my clients. I suspect that most people are similar, and can easily begin to feel overwhelmed, so be aware of this when you're delegating work to others. Don't deluge them, but drip-feed them, and you might find they can do a better job on each individual task.

Next, it's time to bust a great big myth.

A lot of people tell themselves that they can multitask. Wrong. **The ability to multitask effectively is a myth!** MRI brain scans people attempting to multi-task have proven this, going back as far as 2001. (See http://bit.ly/QPbENa if you're interested, or just Google *multitasking myth* for a plethora of evidence.)

Your computer can multitask; you can't. Actually, to be accurate, not even your computer is really multitasking. What it's actually doing is slicing its attention into pieces and focusing on one thing at a time, but switching its focus hundreds of times each second. In computing, this switching between tasks is called a *context switch*. It's quite easy for a computer to do this, but it's very hard for a human. You lose a lot of time putting one thing aside then picking up something else and trying to remember where you got to. So focusing on too many things is a double-whammy: as well as hitting the limits of the human brain to remember everything you're doing in detail, you've also got the time-management hit of getting back into what you were doing before.

It's quite easy to tell if you're trying to do too much at once: if you're feeling frazzled, you can't remember the details of what you're working on, you feel like you're being pulled in a million different ways, and you don't know what to work on next, then you're trying to do too much!

One technique I use to combat this is to use several lists: a yearly list, a monthly list, a weekly list, and a daily list, showing what I need to do to reach my goals. It then becomes easy to plan my work, and to focus only on the things which need doing today.

If you use a tool like **Trello**, at http://www.trello.com, which shows your project as a series of columns with tasks in it, it's easy to tell when you're working on too many things at once. Trello is designed to represent a physical notice board with sticky notes on it, each note representing a task, or a software feature. You put those notes into different columns depending on the progress of each task. You can name the columns however you like, but a column structure like *To Do, In Analysis, In Development, In Testing, Blocked, Done* is common. If you find that you have lots of tasks in any one column then you're in danger of doing too much. The

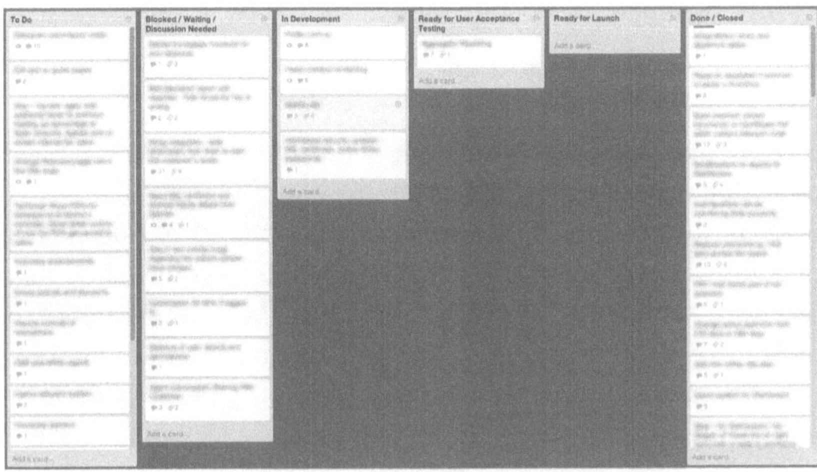

Figure 4. A Trello board from a real-life project. (I have blurred the text on the individual cards, each representing a software feature, to respect confidentiality.) The To Do column on the left shows all the things that aren't yet started, and the Done column on the right shows a nice amount of completed work. The Blocked column, second from left, shows quite a few pieces of work that have stalled. Depending on the size of the team, this might be a warning sign that this project is trying to do too many things at once.

view that Trello gives you is technically known as a *Kanban Board*. The Kanban style of management, where this idea came from, actually suggests that you limit how many cards can be in any column at once. So you might set a limit of three cards in your Analysis column, which is where you put features when you're developing their requirements. Then you can't add a fourth card to this column, and start working on any more Analysis, until one of those original three is done. You'll soon see where you have bottlenecks.

Action Points

Identify if you think you're doing too much. Go on gut feel; that's usually pretty accurate. Try consciously limiting the amount of tasks you work on at any one time. It's better to have one thing properly done than six things messed up!

A useful prioritization technique here is the 80-20 rule: if 80% of your results will come from 20% of the things you do, find that one thing within the 20% that would make the most difference to your project and do that first. Try to work on tasks until they are fully completed, rather than leaving them only partially done. If you're interested in taking the 80-20 principle a lot further, see the books *The 80/20 Principle: The Secret of Achieving More with Less"* by Richard Koch, and *80/20 Sales and Marketing: The Definitive Guide to Working Less and Making More* by Perry Marshall and Richard Koch.

Delegate tasks to others in small batches: one or two things at once, not ten things. They will focus better, and give better results.

Planning your day into time blocks can also help you to focus. You're effectively scripting your day, saying that between 9am and 11am you're going to work on Task 1, then from 11am to 1pm you're going to work on Task 2, etc. By blocking off definite chunks of time you can help to focus your brain. Switch off your phone and email to help you concentrate; it turns out that you can live without email for a couple of hours without dying!

You might have noticed from this description that the problem of trying to do too much is a problem linked to time management. Sharpening your time management skills can help you to focus on not feeling overwhelmed, and on bringing results-getting discipline into your work. The book I recommend on this is *No B.S. Time Management for Entrepreneurs (third edition)*, by Dan Kennedy.

Lack of open discussion with third parties concerning budget

At first glance, "Lack of open discussion with third parties concerning budget" seems like a very odd root cause of failure. Arguably it's not actually a root cause of failure at all, because the real roots lie in how you define quality, but it happens often enough that I want to bring your attention to it.

This root cause of failure is mostly concerned with projects where you're working with a third-party supplier, perhaps with them as a software vendor or a software development team.

Let me illustrate the problem in its most obvious form. Imagine for a moment that you're in the construction industry and you're building a house for a customer. You can build a decent house for $200,000. But for $300,000 you can use much better quality materials—better bricks, better tiles, better windows—and get a much nicer result. And for $400,000 you can do all that plus fit gold accessories in the bathroom, fit longer-lasting kitchen units, a better extractor fan, have a much nicer fireplace, etc. If the budget was right down at only $50,000 you'd be using wood not bricks, or maybe some kind of prefabricated structure.

So there are several different possible budgets to build fundamentally the same house: each produces a house, but of wildly different quality. Unless your customer has specified each and every one of these details of how they want the house to be built, as the builder you're going to have to make some decisions. Even if the customer has said he wants "very high quality windows", or even as detailed as "triple-glazed windows", unless he's given you a make and model number for each window, as the builder you're going to have to decide exactly what you use. You're making decisions on *quality*, based on the *budget* you have.

It's the same deal in software. As a customer, you give the developer a set of requirements and he will come up with a solution. But just like the example of the house, there are lots of ways to meet the requirements. If you want a version of your website that will work on a mobile phone, do you want it to just be a squashed up version of your main website, or do you want it perfectly optimised for the best possible experience on a phone? This would probably involve a redesign of the user interface that appears on the phone, optimizing it for a touch screen rather than a keyboard and mouse. The text and graphics would probably be made clearer for reading on a small screen too. Both approaches would work, in that the customer could use the website, but the quality would be noticeably different. If this was an e-commerce site, perhaps the poorer site would convert 10% of visitors to buyers, and the fully optimised site would convert 20% but be twice as expensive to produce.

So you can meet this challenge of matching quality to budget in one of two ways: either you specify quality to a very, very detailed level, or else you tell your developer your budget and ask them to make the judgment calls. In something as complicated as software development, the developer will probably be balancing a lot of things behind the scenes too, which you don't get to see, regarding testing, internal code design, etc. (There is a half-way house where the developer explains all the trade-offs to you and then you make the calls yourself, but this can be very time-consuming and sometimes fairly technical.)

The first instinct of a customer is to think, "I'm not telling the developer my budget, or that's how much he'll charge me! I'm a hard-ass negotiator; I'm going to keep him in the dark and see if I get a bargain!" You may as well phone a car dealer that sells all makes of car and tell him "I want to buy a car", then see whether he pitches you a Ford or a Ferrari. How the heck would he know what to do? He's not going to sell you the Ferrari for the price of the Ford! Yet in software, it's easier to think you can play this game because you can't touch and feel software, and it's very hard to put a price-tag on it. (Think of your favourite websites or apps: can you even begin to guess how much or how little they cost to develop? Difficult, isn't it!)

A reputable software developer will deliver higher quality for a higher price, and lower quality for a lower price. You won't get a total bargain, but you won't get ripped off either. (If you think you have been ripped off, time to consider going elsewhere!)

This is an area where management styles come into play. Some people would say, "Never reveal your budget, or you'll get taken advantage of." But I can tell you for an absolute fact that I've worked on projects where we could have done a much better job if we'd known how much money we had to spend, simply because we'd have better understood where to focus our time and attention. We would have built in more automated testing, done more manual testing, spent more time on the user interface design, and perhaps worked more closely with graphic designers on each web page rather than just asking them for a template, along with a whole host of other things. In short, we would have changed our approach to deliver something closer to what the customer wanted in their heart-of-hearts The software would have looked better, been more reliable, and probably have met the business goals better.

It's easy for a developer and a customer to talk together about something that everyone can see, like graphic design, but when it comes to software testing the customer will just say "I want it to work", and then pretty much leave the developers to figure out the testing strategy, which is where knowledge of budget is very useful.

Ultimately it's a question of trust and negotiating style: in my opinion, if you trust your developers, just be honest about the budget. Expect your budget to be spent, unless it's wildly over the top. (If you don't want all of your budget to be spent, it's not really your budget!) You can hold a little back for contingency.

A useful technique if you don't want to be up-front about your budget is to get a quotation for the work from your developers, and then say, "What would you do if the budget was increased by 20%? What would you cut if the budget was reduced by 20%?" (There's nothing special about choosing 20%, you could go higher or lower.)

Most developers by default will quote you fairly low, to let them do a reasonable (but not great) job. They don't want to quote high and risk losing the business. But this can mean that when work is underway you'll find lots of quality problems—errors during testing, features not right—and then they'll probably ask for more money to fix it. That will knock you sideways. So why not just be up-front in the first place? You don't want nasty surprises.

Action points

Consider how much you trust your developers. If you trust them, as well as giving them your requirements for the next phase of development, give them your budget too. Ask them if they think it's reasonable. Ask them what they'd do, or cut, if the budget was higher or lower. Explain that you're telling them the budget so that they can make better decisions on quality, and better quality is what you will usually get.

Conclusion: What we achieved in step 5

By now, you should not only have identified the management problems that you think your project has suffered from, but you should have some more knowledge and some practical action steps to start addressing those problems. This is likely to cover some, but not all, of the techniques you will need to turn your project around. We next need to look at specific IT skills and IT skill failures, which is the subject of step 6.

How to fix your IT skills problems

This step is similar to the previous step, in that we'll look at a range of problems in turn, and I'll suggest some practical steps you can take in each case.

These problems are to do with the IT skills that are being used on the project. Skills and people are of course completely interlinked, so we'll talk about the people you'll need in Step 7.

If you're not a technical person yourself, there's a tendency to start to panic or become uneasy when you read about technical topics. On the one hand, I should warn you that there are a few technical terms in this step: I couldn't write about technology without using those terms, but I've kept them to a minimum. On the other hand, there's really nothing to fear here: it's all quite logical and straightforward, and I'm explaining the concepts, rather than the detail, so you'll have no trouble following along.

So let's get started!

Badly defined requirements

I have spent some of my career with the formal job title of Business Analyst, and have spent most of my career using business analysis skills on a day-to-day basis. A good Business Analyst will examine a problem, gain a deep understanding of it, and then define the requirements of the solution needed to solve the problem.

There's a reason that Business Analyst is a job role in its own right: gathering requirements in a full, thorough and accurate manner, balancing the trade-offs between different types of users, is tough.

The British Computer Society (BCS) offers courses and certifications in Business Analyst skills. The International Institute of Business Analysts (IIBA) also does this, and publishes a Business Analysis Body of Knowledge (BABOK) which summarises the skills and techniques of business analysis that are in widespread use. See http://www.iiba.org.

Requirements gathering is concerned with *what* is needed, not *how* it is to be done. (The "how" part is a specification.) A common problem I see is that people don't think about requirements in terms of what they're trying to achieve: they think of requirements immediately in terms of screen designs for software, database changes, and other things that should come later. For example, "We need to give different levels of permission to different users" is a high-level requirement, whereas "We need a screen where I can click on a user name, then tick some boxes to show what permissions he should have" is a specification.

This distinction is important. If we understand *what* you want to achieve, there are probably quite a few ways to do this. Some will be much better than others. For example, there's a story, probably apocryphal, that goes like this. During the space race, when the Americans and the Russians were sending people to the moon, both teams realised they needed a writing tool that would work in zero gravity, because their normal pens wouldn't write upside down. The requirement was "We need to write upside down." The Americans spent millions of dollars developing a pen with a pressurised ink delivery system that would force the ink onto the page even when it was writing upside down. Everyone on the team was amazed with how well they had solved the problem—until they heard that the Russians had solved the same problem by using a pencil. Same requirement, very different specifications for the solution.

A lot of time is wasted when requirements are unclear, because people don't know exactly what problem they are trying to solve, and exactly what the solution must do in order to be successful. They will flounder around, procrastinate, scratch their heads, then deliver the wrong thing, because they don't know what the *right* thing is!

Don't forget to involve as many people in requirements gathering as is sensible and practical. Especially, consider the people who will actually use the software, and people who understand your current business processes, because they may spot flaws or oversights that will need correction. The tendency when developing requirements and specifications for software is to only speak to managers, rather than the people on the ground that actually do the work.

Talk to the people on the ground and you'll often get a very different understanding of where the company currently is, what it does, and what the real day-to-day problems are, where the efficiency gains can be found. Don't see the people at the bottom of the organisation chart as clueless—they're often the most clued-up of all!

Many books have been written on requirements gathering, and it's a real skill that takes experience to master. It took me years to become fully competent at coaxing the real requirements out of people (ie what they *actually* need, not what they *think* they need.)

A good software developer will tell you what he or she needs by way of requirements: what information the developers must have in order to propose a good solution to your problem. A good project assurance person can review the requirements and give a good understanding of whether they are complete, whether they are well-written, and whether they will be easy to develop into successful software.

Action points

Clearly separate your requirements (what you are trying to achieve) from the specification (how you are going to achieve it). You might then see a better, faster, or cheaper way to do the same thing.

You need *written requirements* for every feature that you build. Getting things in writing focusses the mind, and forces you to identify and fix potential problems or areas where there is a tendency to be vague. Try and write the requirements in as much detail as you can. Be specific.

Get everyone in the team to review the requirements, get user input whenever you can, and get the business owner of the software to sign off on the requirement before development begins.

The whole point of written requirements, and reviewing them, is to reduce the number of surprises, where somebody thinks "That isn't what I wanted", or "This won't meet my needs". It's quicker to fix problems when they're still in a Word document than when somebody has spent three weeks developing it in software.

You should use a requirements checklist to make sure you haven't missed anything obvious. The checklist will step you through everything you normally need to consider.

Here's a very simple but powerful tip for your requirements and specifications documents: *number each paragraph*, and keep each paragraph short. Have only one requirement, one main thought, in each paragraph. This makes it so much easier for people to refer to the document when they are commenting on it. It is also much easier to write software tests based on documents where there is only one requirement per paragraph.

Changing requirements that are not handled correctly

Changing requirements are a blessing and a curse. If you think back to the 12 agile principles, the one that you might have had some trouble with was number 2: "Welcome changing requirements, even late in development". Let's be clear: it's a pain in the backside when requirements change! Time and money have been spent developing something that is now no longer needed, or will have to be changed. Having the requirements change isn't much fun for a software developer. So why does the agile principle say to "welcome" changing requirements? Well, it's probably not quite the word that I would have used, especially with my software developer's hat on! I need to give it a little more nuance so that you understand what's going on.

If the requirements do *genuinely* change, because the business environment has changed, or user feedback shows you that something was overlooked, or something really isn't working in practice, then you have to welcome that, and make the change, otherwise your software won't be fit for purpose, and it won't deliver the measurable business benefits. The project will fail. So we have to welcome that change, because if handled correctly it will lead to project success and not to project failure.

However, what we *don't* welcome is poorly-handled changes in requirements. The earlier the requirement changes, the better. It's cheaper to fix a requirement when it's just on paper than when it's been coded into the system. That's why it's important to get requirements reviewed by as many stakeholders as is sensible *before* the requirements are developed.

We also *don't* welcome poorly-controlled change: where the change is not clearly documented and communicated, and the reason for change is not understood. This is because we're left in limbo, not really knowing what we're doing, or why we're doing it, or how this change might affect other parts of the project.

Action points

If you are changing your requirements, make sure the changes are legitimate, and not just made on a whim.

Clearly document the changes, and the reasons for change, and make sure everyone on the project understands these.

Make sure that you assess the full impact of any change request on the business case: does making the change, or not making the change, affect the ability of the project to deliver the measurable business benefits?

Make sure that you assess the full impact of any change request on the software. For example, if a feature in your software changes, you will also need to change the documentation, adjust any user training materials, and make sure that the rest of the software is able to handle the change. For example, if we change from storing a customer's date of birth to just storing their age, a report of users sorted by date of birth is going to break.

Change Management is a well-understood process within the discipline of project management, and PRINCE2, PMP and APMP have things to say on it. If you're suffering because of poor change control in your requirements and your software, it's worth reading up on how to do it properly. (PRINCE2 has an entire theme on handling change.)

Low level of customer/user involvement, or involvement too late

If the software doesn't do what the customer needs it to do, then the project will fail. If users can't use your software, then the software is junk! So what's the easiest way to avoid this problem? **Get customers and users involved early and often.**

It's often not good enough just to ask managers what features should be present and how the software should work; you usually find that the people on the ground who actually use the software, and actually do the job every day, are far better in tune with how the company and its business processes actually work. So make sure you get feedback from those people too: you'll often find problems, hurdles and road-blocks by talking to the people on the ground that you wouldn't find just by talking to managers.

Action points

Ask customers and users to review requirements while they are still on paper, to make sure that you are remaining on track.

Ask customers and users for suggestions as to how to improve the software. Talk to your customers often: face-to-face is best, where possible.

Watch users as they actually use the software. This is called user shadowing. You will soon notice what they find awkward and what you can improve for them.

Consider surveys of users and customers to understand their feelings.

Hold regular demonstrations of new features with users and customers, especially before a new feature is released. If you have a blog, write about the new features. You can then get instant feedback to guide you.

Deliver small sets of features quickly, rather than delivering large batches of features once or twice a year. You will get much more rapid feedback, to stop you going too far off track. This is at the heart of the agile development methodology.

Get users and customers to prioritise the list of which features you develop next, to make sure you are meeting their needs.

Poor communication among customers, developers, and users

At its heart, communication is all about getting everyone working together as one team, focused on project success.

I like software developers to meet customers themselves wherever possible, rather than always working through their managers or a business analyst. This way, the developers can have a structured conversation about the software, and the expectations of the users. If developers can picture the users, understand the users, and put themselves into the shoes of the users, the software will stand a much higher chance of meeting its objectives. This is very important.

Good communication is a skill that can be learned, and there are also some tools and techniques we can use to help us. The advice in this section might seem basic, but think about it, and take it to heart.

Try experimenting with different methods of communication. One of the biggest factors that helps or hinders how effectively we communicate is the choice of medium used. The best methods of communication for developing software are face-to-face, voice calls over telephone, Skype, Zoom, Microsoft Teams, instant message, and email.

Personally I intensely dislike large conference calls, especially when these are audio-only. They are very rarely effective, due to poor sound quality, and lack of clarity on who exactly is speaking. I seek to avoid conference calls wherever possible, and speak to people one-on-one. If you *must* have a conference call, get every person on the call using a separate phone held to their ear or using a headset—*no speaker-phones*! This way the sound clarity will be much better, and at least you'll give yourself a fighting chance of understanding what's being said.

Email can be good where you need to keep a record of what has been said, such as if you are working on the requirements or specification for a certain feature. Email is also good if you need to carefully think about your reply, or need to reply in particular detail, since it gives a precision that face-to-face or voice calls cannot often match. I believe it is better to respect someone by giving them a thoughtful reply by email rather than a few off-the-cuff remarks on the phone. However, if you are exchanging more than two or three emails on a subject, it's best to have a voice call or a face-to-face meeting. After the call, write up the notes, and send them to the other person to make sure you both agree on what was said.

Personally, I always schedule my voice calls via email or instant message, to avoid playing phone tag with someone. It also gives me time to prepare properly for the call, which is a basic courtesy to the other person. Never underestimate the power of good preparation! I would encourage you to *always* schedule your calls, and not just call someone out of the blue, unless it is a dire emergency. Your calls will be much more productive this way, and your time management will improve too.

Knowing *how much* to communicate is also a skill. Some people are windbags who never shut up, and other people have to have information dragged out of them like a secret service interrogation! Pay attention to getting this balance right.

Your job as a leader is to keep channels of communication open, and make sure that developers, users and customers all talk to each other, and all talk to you as appropriate. To keep things manageable, you can appoint representatives from each of these groups: developers, users, and customers. Then you can work mainly with the representatives.

PRINCE2 talks about this, and has the project controlled by what it calls a Project Board, which contains one or more Senior Users and Senior Suppliers. It's a good structure, and in practice it works well.

Action points

For every communication, actively consider whether it would be most productive face-to-face, by voice, by email, or by instant message.

Evaluate your communications, after they have taken place, to see whether you chose the most effective method of communicating. In this way you can learn to improve.

Consider a software tool to synchronise communication. A lot of my clients love **Trello**, at http://www.trello.com. This gives a simple on-screen representation of a series of cards that can be moved into different columns to show the status of an item. It also allows additional notes, with a time and date stamp, to be kept on each item, and it lets you assign items to specific people. It's very simple to use, and can give very powerful results.

If you have to make a lot of calls, software such as **TimeTrade** might be useful. See http://www.timetrade.com. Timetrade allows online scheduling of appointments, and can synchronise with Google Calendar.

Depending on your project, consider sending a regular email to communicate the project status and to get feedback. This might be based on the Highlight Report that you and your senior team are using to control the project.

Regular demonstrations are a good way to keep the different stakeholders on your project communicating with each other.

Use of the wrong technology
(immature, outdated, not fit for purpose)

You usually have to choose your technology at the start of the project, and then stick with it. This means that if you get it wrong you're in for a lot of trouble.

Most of the time you should choose a mainstream technology. This will mean there are lots of people who know how to use it (so you can hire them at an affordable price), there will be lots of people available in future to support it (very important, don't overlook this), and the technology will provide a good set of stable and reliable features to build on.

If you choose a new or immature technology, you won't find many people who can use it, it might fall out of favour and become impossible to develop and support, and it might not allow you to do everything you need to do. (On the other hand, it might be a massive shortcut to success, but you're making a brave choice!)

If you choose an outdated technology, it will be hard to find people who want to work on it, and soon it will no longer be supported by its vendor, which can lead to big problems if things go wrong, especially when it comes to security patches to guard against the latest vulnerabilities.

The problem with technology is that it gets old quickly. Today's mainstream is tomorrow's outdated product. For example, in 2006 I developed an application in a programming language called Ruby on Rails, version 1. This was cutting edge at the time! I stand by that decision, because it made writing the application very simple and quick compared to the other choices that were common at the time. However, as I write this, Ruby on Rails is still going strong, but it's now at version 6. Version 1 is no longer supported for security fixes, and a lot of the latest cool web tricks are very hard or impossible to pull off. Really, if serious changes were needed to this application, it would need to largely be rewritten.

Sadly that's just the price of progress though, and there's not much you can do about it, other than choosing a mainstream technology that doesn't look like it's going away.

The biggest and most established technologies, that are fairly safe for you to stick to in the case of most projects, are:

- Microsoft C#, Java, Ruby on Rails or PHP as your programming language.
- Linux or Windows as your operating system.
- SQL Server, Oracle, MySQL or PostgreSQL as your choice of database.

Having said this, each of these technologies has times when it is a great choice, and times when it is a bad choice. If you are in doubt, check this with an experienced technologist or your project assurance person.

Action points

Think: do you need to change technology?

If you need to change, is it too late to change technology? Often it is too late, but sometimes you can make a change, either immediately or by starting introducing new technologies as appropriate and phasing out the old technologies over time.

Poor development practices

Software development is now a very mature and well-understood field. A lot is known about best practice and bad practice, and huge numbers of books have been written on this. Agile development practices are the current flavour-of-the-month, and have been for quite a few years now, with good reason.

It's hard to give a definitive guide to good and bad practice in the space I have here, and a lot of the discussion is for hardcore techies only! However, a few signs of good practice to look out for in software development are:

- Clear, *written* requirements and specification.
- Structured and formal testing, including automated testing (see the section "Poor software testing" below).
- Frequent progress reports.
- Use of known design patterns when designing the system.
- Proper handling of change.
- Proper defect reporting and correction .
- Developers who are up to date on latest practice by receiving training and going to conferences.

A lot of problems come from developers who do not fully understand your requirements, or do not understand your business domain. (For example, in the case of a travel insurance company that I have worked with, their first two sets of developers just couldn't wrap their heads around travel insurance, and in the absence of clear written specifications they were unable to produce anything with any business value.)

Developers forced to work overtime will often make mistakes due to the stress and the pressure of work. I once saw a project for a very large European telecoms company that was running late, and the response was to get the developers to work late and to work 7 days a week. As the developers got more and more tired, the mistakes just piled up. Eventually a catastrophic mistake was made, and as a result the manager was fired. Only then was the project approach re-evaluated. The moral of the story: **it's better to cut the scope than to work people into the ground.**

Related to this is the number of people working on a project. Double the number of developers will *not* produce double the work! They will get in the way of each other, and their work will conflict. They will also spend time waiting for each other. You will accomplish much more with two great developers than with ten mediocre developers. (This is why a lot of outsourcing to companies who provide a huge number of people, using cheap workers, often fail to get good results.)

Action points

Look at the list above, and evaluate your developers on it. If you're not sure how to do this, check with an experienced technologist or your project assurance person.

Train your developers to know when to ask for help. Even if your requirements and specifications are excellent, there will still be unanswered questions. Also decide with them on how they should ask you for help. Will you have structured meetings on a regular basis, or make yourself available by email? Choose a method that doesn't suck up too much of your time.

If you have meetings, make sure you run them properly. Consider carefully who to invite and who not to invite—too many cooks can spoil the broth. Also, create and publish your agenda in advance, so that everyone can be prepared. You should *expect* everyone to come prepared, too!

Consider having frequent discussions with development teams, customers and users. This can solve a lot of problems that would otherwise be put down to poor development practices. Sometimes a short daily meeting is appropriate. (In agile this is called a Stand Up meeting, because it is usually held standing up, as a means of making sure people keep things short and to the point.)

Poor software testing

Software testing is a greatly-undervalued discipline, and usually when a project starts falling behind time the first thing that gets cut is the testing. In reality, testing is all about delivering quality, and quality should never be the first thing to be cut. **Always consider cutting scope, and doing less, rather than cutting testing and therefore cutting the quality of features.**

At its heart, testing is about having confidence that the software is fit for purpose: confidence that it will actually do what you think it will do. And really this boils down to levels of confidence: each testing activity will give you a new level of confidence in the accuracy of the system. You then have to trade-off between quality and budget: more money invested in testing should lead to higher quality. (And yes, I used the phrase "money invested", not "money spent", because good testing usually is an investment, and it pays off in terms of quality and customer satisfaction.)

There are two types of testing I want to consider here: testing from the point of view of the software development team, and testing from your point of view as a client and business owner.

First, let's take a look at software testing done by the software development team.

Ideally, the development team should be taking the requirements and specification documents and writing a set of test scripts based on this. The way that I usually work, each small paragraph in the documents becomes one or more separate tests. For example, there might be a requirement that says "The admin user should be able to turn the Facebook Sharing feature on and off." There would then be two tests written, "When I turn the feature off then the feature is off", and "When I turn the feature on then the feature is on".

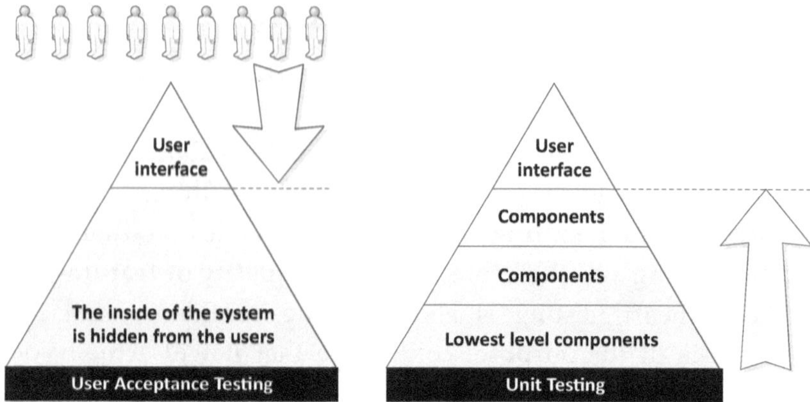

Figure 5. The two main approaches to software testing. In User Acceptance Testing, the users work by testing the User Interface (for a website this will be their web browser), and they don't see the inside of the system. By contrast, unit testing is usually automated, done by the developers, and makes sure that each layer of components is tested so that the layers above it are built on firm foundations. Unit testing usually doesn't go up as far as the user interface, since it can be hard to automate those tests.

If you do not have written test scripts, your testing is unlikely to be thorough, is likely to be ad hoc and random, and is likely to let lots of bugs slip through the net and make their way into the launched product.

Testing is a specialist discipline, and there are a surprising number of qualifications for testers and test managers. While pretty much everyone can notice a massive crash-and-burn failure, a lot of software defects are more subtle, and require skilled testers who understand how to push a system to find more subtle problems. For example, putting a quotation mark into a text field can sometimes cause a system to fail, or even to allow a malicious user to exploit a security flaw and write directly to your database!

Testing is often an entry-level job in the world of software, and sometimes gets looked down upon. Don't look down on testing or testers. Testing is a worthwhile and respectful profession, and testers require the respect of yourself as a manager, and the development team, in order to do their best work.

If your testers aren't picking up problems, then check they have enough time, and that they are suitably skilled. Check what types of testing they are doing, and ask to see their test scripts (the written records of what they are testing). An experienced technologist or project assurance person will tell you whether the test scripts are likely to be adequate.

There are two basic ways to test. If you imagine software as a pyramid, with the user sitting on top and the real low-level guts of the software on the base of the pyramid, then broadly speaking you can either do *User Acceptance Testing*, which is top-down and starts with the user actually using the software, or you can do Unit Testing which is bottom-up and starts at the bottom by testing the smallest components at the lowest level in the system, then testing the next layer of components that build on these, and aiming to make sure that each layer of the system is built on correct foundations. Both types of testing are very useful, and both should be used on a good project.

Behaviour-Driven Development - BDD

There are many different ways to write test scripts. A modern approach to test scripts, that I have used to great effect on projects that have delivered millions of dollars of benefits, is called BDD, which stands for Behaviour-Driven Development. (BDD is actually about a lot more than just test scripts, but that's all I'll focus on here.) I like this approach because it's very simple to understand, for technical people and business people, yet it's powerful enough to get results.

All a BDD test consists of is a description of what you're trying to test, a few steps, and then what you expect to see at the end. This is expressed as a "Given, When, Then" scenario. For example:

Scenario: I can turn the Facebook Sharing feature on
Given I am in the admin console
When I turn the Facebook Sharing feature on
And I go to the page where the user can share on Facebook
Then I see the Facebook Sharing feature is on

It really is as simple as that. You can build up a large set of tests quite quickly like this, that anyone can check and understand.

Regression testing

Another form of testing that the software development team should be doing is called regression testing. I usually think of hypnotists regressing people to past lives when I think about regression testing, but sadly it's not quite as interesting! All it means is that when you introduce new features, you want to make sure that the old features haven't been broken. For example, if I decide I no longer want to ask a customer for their email address, will the screen that displays the user details still work correctly if it can't find an email address?

When a change in one part of the software affects another part of the software we call it a dependency, and these dependencies can be very hard to predict ahead of time. (Something about the human brain just doesn't seem geared up for thinking in this way, especially when the system is complicated.)

You might have spotted a problem here. Each new feature needs a lot of tests writing, to make sure that it is properly working. And as more features are added, the amount of regression testing to make sure that the old features are still working is getting larger and larger. Surely testing will end up taking more and more time and become ever-more costly, won't it?

Automated testing

Fortunately, there's a solution to the drudgery, fatigue and human error of human testing, and it's called automated testing. You can get the computer to do a lot of the testing for you. It can happily enter values onto web pages, check for responses, and do all manner of things. Some automated testing, called unit testing, is done by developers, and looks in detail at each little part of the code. Other automated tests, that mimic the action of a real life user, can be written by the testers (if they have the skills) using technologies with odd names such as Cucumber and Gherkin.

It's more important that you grasp the concept rather than the specific technologies here. The idea is that the *test suite* (i.e. the list of tests) is programmed into the computer, and then any time that changes are made to the software, the automated tests can be run by the computer, and any problems can be found quickly without relying on avoiding human error. This is a *very powerful concept*. Automated testing takes time to set up, and in the short-term it *will* slow you down. However, as the software grows larger, it acts as a vital safety net against mistakes. If you think your project is going to be around for a long time, and you've got the up-front budget to do it, automated testing is a discipline that your software team should be getting into.

User Acceptance Testing - UAT

Finally in this section, I want to look at the testing that you and your team should be doing as business owners. This testing happens when the software development team delivers you a new feature, and it is called User Acceptance Testing, or UAT. This is where you make sure that the new software or the new feature actually meets your needs. The truth is that very few customers know how to do proper User Acceptance Testing, and so they often accept software that is not fit for purpose, simply because they did not find the problems within it, and didn't realise it was defective.

But hang on—shouldn't you trust the testers on your development team? Well, yes, to a point. But they can make mistakes. Also, they can misunderstand the problem your software is trying to solve, since they don't know the subject matter as well as you. For example, on a website that sells travel insurance, they might not realise that you can only sell a policy up to 90 days into the future, if for some reason they haven't seen that part of the specification, or have forgotten to write a test for it. This would be very obvious to you if you were a travel insurance business owner and had negotiated the agreement with the insurance underwriter, and so you would want to test for it.

You will also find that software developers and testers don't normally use the system in the same ways that a standard user or customer (or you) would use it.

The usual approach to UAT, where the customer checks whether the software is fit for purpose, is for the customer to just play around with the software for a while, find any obvious mistakes, and then consider the software as acceptable. I would urge you at least to add a bit more structure to this. You might not have the time or skill to write a full set of test cases, but at least make a list of the general things you want to test, and break them down into a little more detail. Concentrate on the most important things. A mind map is a good tool for creating this, since it lets you drill down into whatever level of detail you want. Again **XMind** could be your friend here.

There are two main paths through the system that you will want to test: the positive path and the negative path. The positive path (or happy path) means that you are entering all the right values in the right places, and the system is doing what it should do. The negative path is where you deliberately enter bad values, or miss things out, in an attempt to break the system or see how it will cope with errors and failure. A common failing is only to test the positive path, or to insufficiently test the negative path—there are usually a lot of ways to break a system!

A key to success in User Acceptance Testing (UAT) is making sure that the right people from your company are doing the testing. It's often best to ask the actual people who will be using the software to test it, and also the people who know the results they are expecting to see (for example, if you are testing insurance premium calculations, the people who know how to do those calculations manually are the people from your company who should test this). Although managers can be good at user acceptance testing, you should try to involve the people on the ground if you can.

If your new system is to replace a current system, then it's best if the users of the current system do some of your testing, because they will be able to spot if anything important has been missed.

Action points

If you think testing is failing to find enough problems, you should check the test scripts your development team is using. Just the fact that the development team knows that you are on the case by asking to see the test scripts, or asking to regularly review them, will keep their minds focused.

I would strongly encourage you to look at putting automated testing in place on your projects if you can, especially if the software is likely to be around for quite a long time, and will be changed and updated during the course of its life (something that will happen to almost all pieces of software).

Consider your approach to User Acceptance Testing. Do you need to tighten up your procedures on how you test software before you will accept it as ready for use?

If your software is being built by a third-party provider, out-sourced and/or off-shored, you will want to do one or both of the following:

1. Send someone to audit the testing procedures and methods used by your software vendor. Are they doing unit tests? Automated test? How are they doing these? Do you have confidence in them?

2. Treat the system as a black box (where you don't know what's inside it) and run your own detailed User Acceptance Tests on the software when you receive it, to make sure it is fit for purpose.

Poor reporting and handling of bugs and defects

As a software developer myself, one of my huge bugbears is the awful quality of the problem reports I receive. When I worked on a very large system I once got an email that simply said: "Your software doesn't work. Please let me know when you have fixed it." Er, sorry, could you be a bit more vague, please?! How the heck am I supposed to even get started with investigating that? (In this particular case I phoned the guy, soon discovered that his computer had about ten different viruses on it that were ripping its guts out, and closed the case!)

As a little note on terminology, problems with software used to be called bugs, because the original computers that relied more on mechanical actions sometimes used to get actual insects trapped in them that would cause problems. The term bug is still in common use, but as the IT industry has tried to professionalise, and has taken on a lot of concepts from the lean manufacturing and Six Sigma movements, the term "defect" has also come into common usage. Bug, defect, glitch, they all mean the same thing. (Pain, usually!)

So first of all you've got to get people reporting bugs properly, and second you've got to manage those reports. There are good techniques to help you here, and we'll look at those now.

The important thing that you need to know about how a developer goes about fixing a problem is that they will almost always look to *reproduce* it for themselves, so that they can see what's wrong, then fix it. So **you need to give the development team the information they need—usually a clear set of steps—to be able to reproduce the defect.**

Some defects are really hard to reproduce. As developers, we call these phase-of-the-moon bugs, because that's the only thing we can think of that might be causing the problem! Of course, it's more likely to be the unique coming together of a set of circumstances that you haven't yet identified that's causing the problem.

A good bug report is all about being precise and accurate, as best as you can. Sometimes you can't remember exactly what you were doing, but just give as much info as you can.

Sometimes it's easiest to record your screen, using Camtasia or Screenflow, as you demonstrate the defect, and then send the developers the video.

The next two pages will give you the "gold standard" for how you go about reporting bugs. They're your "cut out and keep" guide.

You'll find that if you don't report bugs in manner similar to this then your developers will get a bit tetchy and non-productive, because it soon gets irritating trying to track down problems when you're really not sure what you're looking for. Depending on how your developers are contracted to work for you, they might be afraid to speak up and tell you that your bug reporting is shoddy, so really do your best to get this right for them.

Elements of a good bug report

When you're writing a bug report, be sure to give information on the following:

- A short but descriptive title, eg "Error 500 received when clicking Submit on purchase page".

- The system you noticed the problem on (can just be "test system" or "live system").

- A version number for the software, if there is one (usually on web applications there isn't).

- Some kind of classification for how serious you think the problem is. (See the table below.)

- The date and time of day that you noticed the bug (so the developer knows where to look in the system logs to check for an error message, because each log entry has a timestamp).

- Can you reproduce this defect? Every time, sometimes, or are you unable to reproduce it?

- A step-by-step guide to reproduce the problem – note down everything you did.

- What you *expected* to happen if the system was working correctly.

- What *actually* happened.

- A screenshot (or several) if appropriate (or a video).

- Any error message you saw, eg "502 Bad Gateway".

- If your system is a web application, copy and paste the URL of the web page where the error is occurring, eg http://www.test.com/admin/users?id=123.

- Give your contact details so that the developer can contact you for more information if required.

If you need more information on writing defect reports, you'll find a good and detailed explanation of how to write a bug report here: http://bit.ly/1pHqBBm

When it comes to software for tracking bugs, there are lots of good bug tracking software applications to choose from. I like **Lighthouse**, a web-based tool. It's quite simple to use, but gives you all the features you need. http://lighthouseapp.com

There are much more complicated tools, but I prefer a simple tool because people are more likely to be able to use it, so they might actually use it. A tool that nobody uses is not worth having!

Another popular tool is **Fogbugz**: https://www.fogbugz.com.

You can even use **Trello** itself to track bugs if your project is relatively small: http://www.trello.com.

It's useful to classify bugs into various levels of severity, and then to agree on a **Service Level Agreement (SLA)** for how quickly those bugs will be fixed. Note that you don't have to fix every single bug: minor things might be too time-consuming to fix, or some things might be in a very fragile part of the code and might be best just left alone.

Severity Level	Description	Target time to fix
1	A critical show-stopper that prevents the system from running.	4 hours
2	A serious failure in one part of the system.	24 hours
3	Inconvenient, but not urgent to fix.	5 working days
4	Minor or cosmetic, such as a spelling mistake.	14 working days

Figure 6. A commonly used set of severity levels for defects. This basic classification works well on most projects.

Personally I don't like to have many bugs open and unresolved at any one time, otherwise the software starts to get messy and users and developers lose confidence in it—a disaster. This is really about the broken windows theory, developed in criminology, which states that it is better to maintain an urban environment in a pleasant condition, rather than tolerating broken windows, which can bring about a slippery slope where people stop caring about their environment and are willing to escalate to more serious vandalism and crime. In other words, if people think the software is bad, and you do nothing to dispel that myth, they are more likely to stop caring about making the software better, and quality will be irreparably ruined.

Target time to fix a bug can never be absolutely guaranteed, because some problems are very difficult to investigate and fix, but it's good to have a target so that everyone has the same expectations of priority and urgency.

One final problem I'd like to address here is a common problem on many projects: fixing one defect, or adding a new feature, will cause something to break somewhere else. Sometimes it feels like you're playing Whac-A-Mole—as soon as you bash one bug another one pops up! This is usually a symptom of something quite seriously wrong. It often happens after the software has been in use for quite a while and has been repeatedly upgraded. If it happens on a new project, that's a very serious concern. If you're constantly finding new problems, the software code is likely to be in a seriously bad way: unstructured, everything depending on everything else, and the developers walking on eggshells trying not to change anything. It is also likely that the testing is not as thorough as it could be: time to check those test scripts and regression testing strategies.

Automated testing can help a lot in this case, because it gives the developers confidence to know that they will at least get an early warning if they have introduced a new problem. It's often a long, slow road to get out of this kind of problem, and it usually involves re-engineering the code base over a long period of time, and making incremental improvements as the developers go along to start making things better.

To give you one very common example: over a period of time there might get to be some very similar code in several different places within the software; when a change is needed it then needs to be changed in all these places, and you can be pretty sure that something is going to be missed. One of the changes the developers might make to improve things is to consolidate all these pieces of code into a single piece of code, removing duplication and making the software easier to maintain.

Action points

Develop a strategy for how to classify and handle bugs, such as using the table I've given here.

Get a good bug tracker, and make sure everyone knows how to use it. Stick with it, and use it for all bugs. If in doubt, start with **Lighthouse**. It's simple and effective. http://lighthouseapp.com.

Make sure everyone knows what is needed to write a good bug report, and then see that they always write their bug reports like this.

Schedule a periodic review of bugs in the software. You might incorporate this into your Highlight Report for tracking the project.

Keep a track of the number of bugs found and fixed each month. If this number starts going up, be concerned, because you could be entering Whac-A-Mole territory, and it's good to have an early warning of that before things get too bad.

Inability to handle the project's complexity

When I was an undergraduate studying computer science, one of my first ever lectures was by a grizzled old veteran of the commercial computer programming world who'd sought refuge in academia. One of the first things he said to us was, *"Your entire life in software development will be about the battle against complexity."* And he was exactly right. Handling complexity is very, very difficult. The human brain just isn't wired to cope with it.

The real key to handling complexity is just to avoid complexity wherever you can. Simplify, simplify, simplify!

If 80% of the benefit comes from 20% of the features—and it usually does—then see which features you can simplify or remove. Reduce your scope and reduce your problems!

Project management methodologies such as PRINCE2 help you to avoid complexity, by defining a simple but comprehensive set of reports, so you should look at those.

As an example of how to reduce complexity, I have often received requests from customers for "a demo system that we can play around with or show to a prospective client". This almost always translates to "Spend a week preparing something, and somebody will log in once if you're lucky, use it for 2 minutes, and then never use it again". But you still have the complexity of having to manage a whole new system, keep it updated, keep it secure, etc. It's not worth it. So evaluate those types of requests very carefully. Make life easy, not complicated.

Complication can often arise from people as well as from technology. Complicated reporting lines for staff, complicated sign-off procedures, and unclear leadership can all gum you up. Try to simplify your project structure, for reporting, sign-off, and specification, to give yourself a clearer run at success.

Action points

When a request comes in, evaluate it specifically for complexity. Will it make your life simpler or more complicated? If it makes life more complicated, try and simplify it or reject it.

See if you can reduce your project's scope, or make some features simpler, in order to keep complexity down.

Check that your processes for sign-offs and reporting are clear and simple.

Software projects get very complicated very quickly. Be constantly on the lookout for complexity and the opportunity to simplify.

Conclusion: What we achieved in step 6

Wow, that was a lot of words, and I really only barely scratched the surface of each topic. I've given you a rough map of the territory, of the sorts of problems you will see under each major problem heading, and the sorts of solutions you can think about and take action on.

Now you will have a better idea of what you need to investigate in further depth in order to turn your project around, and you can start taking action to fix things. You might well need to talk these issues over with your software team, and a technical expert or project assurance person. The devil is in the detail with this kind of work.

In the spirit of saving the best until last, in the final step we'll look at the single most important part of software success: *people*.

Get the right people on the project

People are vital to success on a software project. The right people, using a bad methodology, will still come up with something decent. The wrong people, using a great methodology, will still produce rubbish. I've seen enough outsourcing firms full of cheap human robots blindly following a method to tell you 100% that this is true!

First of all I'm going to cover *you*, the senior leader or entrepreneur, because you are vital to the success of the project. Then I'm going to cover the three main types of people you're going to need: developers, testers, and a project manager. I'm also going to explain the role of project assurance: a person experienced in both software development *and* software projects, who provides you with guidance. This is a little-known role which can massively increase your chance of success and massively decrease your chance of failure.

You: The senior leader, entrepreneur, or executive

You have a key part to play in the success of the project, because you are at the top of the tree, as the figurehead, directing the action. The same goes for your senior leaders.

PRINCE2 says that there are four key characteristics that the members of the project board (i.e. the senior leadership of the project) should have:

1. Authority
2. Credibility
3. Ability to delegate
4. Availability

Since you and your senior leaders are a vital part of success, I strongly urge you to get a copy of the PRINCE2 manual, called "Managing Successful Projects with PRINCE2", read the chapter on Organisation, and also see the appendix on the roles and responsibilities that are required to stand a good chance of success.

Ability to delegate, or not, is a problem I often see. As a senior leader, you might be too busy to look into the detail of the project, or quite frankly you might be a big-picture person and not a detail-person. Any IT project will require a lot of time from the business people, so if you can't give this time yourself then you'll need to delegate to somebody, preferably someone who is detail-oriented, decisive, and has the power (given to them by you) to make decisions. That last part is important: the best business owners of a product will make good, timely decisions. A lack of involvement by senior business people can often contribute to either slowing down the project or derailing it altogether. The last thing you want is a "Key Man" problem, where you are the linchpin of the entire project but you don't have any time to devote to it.

The #1 personal quality you'll need in order to succeed is the ability to manage your time so that you have the time to properly focus on the project. Your project will need detailed attention from you and your team to be a success. If you don't have time, delegate.

Your project is going to need someone closely involved who is a real "detail person". If you're a senior business leader, an entrepreneur, or a "big picture guy", that might not be you! There's no shame in this, but if you haven't got the sort of personality where you like to go deep into the detail then you *must* work closely with someone who is detail-oriented. This could be either an employee or an outsider. Requirements, specifications, and User Acceptance Testing are all about detail.

Developers

As I've said earlier, a good software developer is ten times as productive as a poor developer. In fact, really bad developers can have negative productivity, as somebody else needs to go and correct their mistakes!

I really feel strongly that if you want success on your software projects then you need the best developers, or at least very good developers, so I want to spend a minute to examine the research findings on this subject.

The well-known and respected author on software creation, Steve McConnell, wrote an article in 2008 called "Productivity Variations Among Software Developers and Teams: The Origin of 10x". In this article he reviewed some of the studies that have come out since as far back as 1968, which confirm that the difference in productivity between the best and the worst programmers is at least 10 to 1. The article later went on to form the basis of a chapter in a book published by O'Reilly, a respected technical publisher. Here are two key extracts from his article:

> In years since the original study, the general finding that "There are order-of-magnitude [10 to 1] differences among programmers" has been confirmed by many other studies of professional programmers (Curtis 1981, Mills 1983, DeMarco and Lister 1985, Curtis et al. 1986, Card 1987, Boehm and Papaccio 1988, Valett and McGarry 1989, Boehm et al 2000).

> When you think about it, this just makes sense. We've all known people who are exceptional students, exceptional athletes, exceptional artists, exceptional parents--these differences are just part of the human experience; why would we expect software development to be any different?

In 2011, after being challenged on the accuracy of his first article, McConnell wrote a second article, called "Origins of 10X – How Valid is the Underlying Research?". Here are a couple of quotations from this article:

> As I reviewed these citations once again in writing this article, I concluded again that they support the general finding that there are 10x productivity differences among programmers. The studies have collectively involved hundreds of professional programmers across a spectrum of programming activities. Specific differences range from about 5:1 to about 25:1, and in my judgment that collectively supports the 10x claim.

> Having said that, the body of research that supports the 10x claim is as solid as any research that's been done in software engineering... The fact that no studies have produced findings that contradict the 10x claim provides even more confidence in the 10x claim. When I consider the number of studies that have been conducted, in aggregate I find the research to be not only suggestive, but conclusive – which is rare in software engineering research.

These findings completely fit with my own practical experience and observation. If you can find someone five times better than average, you're not going to have to pay them five times as much, so recruiting the best developers you can will actually give you a positive return on investment. I think you get the point by now!

If you're interested in an overview of the current state of knowledge in software engineering—basically everything the world knows about software engineering—then you'll find it in the freely-available *Guide to the Software Engineering Body of Knowledge*, known as SWEBOK, published by the Institute of Electrical and Electronics Engineers (IEEE). There are some good diagrams to give you an overview of the state of the art, and can just skim-read and look at the diagrams to get some value. If nothing else, it will make you realise just how much a good developer is expected to know! For SWEBOK, see https://bit.ly/3lhWmzY.

You should aim for small teams of great people, rather than large teams of second-rate and third-rate people. Let me tell you a story to illustrate this.

On a project I worked on recently, we had two specific features we were looking at, and we thought that each would take four weeks to develop, so eight weeks in total. The project had two developers, both of whom are absolutely first-rate, world-class software developers. After some deep thought, they realised they could re-use some other parts of the system, and make a few tweaks, and they delivered both features in one week, not eight. The tweaks were not obvious, and most people would have missed them. But *they* didn't.

So what were the benefits here? A saving of seven weeks for a start! That's seven weeks to work on other things, and seven weeks earlier to market for the new features.

And how do the economics of this stack up?

If the good developers were five times more expensive than the weak developers, but worked seven times more quickly, that's an obvious win, because you've saved money. If the total cost of the good developers was the same as the total cost of the bad developers, you've still gained seven weeks, which is usually a big win. Even if the good developers were to cost more (which over the long run they won't), you'll still come out ahead because the software will be of higher quality, with fewer defects and problems. The good developers will help to guide you to success.

But there's a hidden benefit here too. The best developers are much better at writing *code that is easy to test*. A big problem is that code also gets harder and harder to maintain over time, and it usually gets to be a proper mess that nobody wants to go anywhere near, as various people have hacked around at it over the years. The best developers will keep the code cleaner and more maintainable, and in a longer project, or a project where you hope to keep changing the software over time (e.g. a lot of websites fall into this category) this is a massive advantage that just gets bigger over time.

So **don't be immediately lured by the promise of low hourly rates**, especially those more prevalent with offshore development teams. I'm not saying that you should never outsource or you should never offshore, but I'm suggesting that you look at the quality of the *specific* developers you will be working with, and at their experience. **You'll have a much easier time working with the best developers, you'll get better results, and you'll keep your sanity!** Believe me, along with being an utterly false economy, working with poor quality developers is an ongoing and living hell! *I don't over-state my case here.*

One case where out-sourcing and offshoring works particularly well is for small, simple pieces of work costing under $500. I use a website called **Upwork** for this, at http://www.upwork.com, and have achieved very good results. I won't go into it now, because it's a topic all to itself, but you can easily access a wide variety of good professionals, post your job, ask them to tender for the work, get star ratings on the providers who give you a quote, choose a quote, and pay for the work either at an hourly rate or a fixed price.

Give me a small crack team over a large crap team any day! You'll have fewer problems synchronizing a small team, fewer personnel issues to deal with, fewer people to be kept informed or have their nose pushed out of joint, and everything just runs more smoothly.

So how do you recruit a good development team? It depends on whether you're recruiting individual people, or hiring a specialist firm.

If you're recruiting individual candidates, ask them to do a *technical test*. A good way to do this is to set a simple-to-understand and short programming challenge, and then have one or two of your talented developers sit with the candidate while the candidate codes the solution. The experienced developers can ask questions and see how the candidate thinks. For example, do they think about how to handle cases where the data is missing or bad? Do they spot the weird and unusual cases that will lead to failure, and code defensively to avoid them? Of course, you will also see which projects the developer has worked on previously, but be careful to ask them what *exactly* they themselves did: most software development is a team effort, and if you're looking for someone to do the database work you might not want to choose a candidate who specialised in the pretty-pictures graphical part of a previous website.

It is possible to get certifications in most of the major programming languages, although they aren't needed in the same way that a doctor needs a medical license in order to practice. (You might argue that a more formal path of training, apprenticeship and qualifications would be a good thing in IT.)

I'm not going to list the qualifications here, since it really depends on what software programming languages you're using and what your project is trying to achieve, but if you do a bit of searching on the web you'll soon find the qualifications that would be useful. Here's a tip: go on the job websites and look what qualifications other people trying to recruit these developers are asking for. Just Google "IT Jobs" (no quote marks) to find a jobs board for your particular country.

If you're hiring a specialist firm, in some ways it's not too different from hiring any specialist firm, such as a marketing agency, a PR firm or an outsourced manufacturing partner. You'll ask for references from previous clients, examples of past work, check reviews of their work (for example reviews of their apps on the various app stores), and—crucially—see how much they know about your particular industry and your particular problem. You can also work this process backwards: if you see a good piece of software that you want to replicate, then find out who was responsible for developing it and contact them directly. There are some very specialist software development firms these days, so you might be able to find the perfect partner.

However you hire your development team, the proof is in the pudding: you won't know how good they are until they start delivering results. So you want them to start delivering results as soon as possible so that you can either gain confidence or fire them quickly, without wasting too much time or money.

A project that's run in an agile manner, where you deliver small pieces of software often, is a good way to test a new development team. It soon becomes clear whether you can work with them, and whether they are any good or not, and you only have to wait a few weeks to find out, rather than waiting a year during which the team hasn't delivered anything.

Another good way to test a development team is to do a proof-of-concept. The aim is just to do something small, quickly, that proves general competence. It's sometimes useful to choose one of the more difficult pieces of the project for the proof-of-concept, because if a development team can't do that then either you'll need to change your team or re-think your project. If you choose something easy for the proof-of-concept, it sets a low bar so it's quite difficult to judge the real competence of the team.

It's often hard to change development teams once a project is underway. But it's not impossible. A new development team will quite likely want to throw everything away though and start again, which might or might not be the best course of action. You've got to know when to cut your losses, and that comes with experience over lots of software projects. It's a very delicate decision to make, and a good project assurance person can give you the benefit of their experience on this one.

Testers

Software testing is often overlooked, and software testers are often considered the poor relation of developers. This is a great shame, because testing ensures quality.

It's worth the time to get a good and experienced software tester involved in your project.

The best testers have a specific mind-set. They are hugely detail-oriented, and are also able to focus on what can sometimes be repetitive and boring work (although test automation can help to relieve testers of the drudgery, and allow them to focus on more creative testing.)

There are a surprising amount of qualifications available in software testing. It's an area that lends itself well to formal training, techniques, and knowledge that's broadly similar and transferable no matter what environment or programming language you're in, which partially explains this. The qualifications used to be called ISEB, but are now the International Software Testing Qualifications Board (ISTQB).

The advice for hiring testers is similar to the advice for hiring developers.

Project manager

In *Improving IT Project Outcomes by Systematically Managing and Hedging Risk*, a 2009 IDC report by Dana Wiklund and Joseph C. Pucciarelli, the authors, found that **54% of projects fail due to poor project management**. That's huge! So it's clearly important to have a good project manager! Look for qualifications such as PRINCE2, PMP or APMP. Also, check the project manager's experience on projects of a similar size to yours, or delivering a similar sort of product or benefit.

Personally, I think that the best project managers on software projects have often been software developers themselves. This isn't a hard and fast rule though. Some very good project managers have never been developers, and a lot of developers wouldn't necessarily class themselves as a "people person", and can lack project management skills. But developing software is weird: it has its own rhythm, and its own subtle signs of success and failure. You learn to pick up on those signs as a developer, in a way that a non-developer wouldn't. Considering my own experience, since I've developed a lot of software myself, good luck trying to pull the wool over my eyes with bad estimates, poor decision-making, slow progress or poor-quality work. I've been in those shoes, so it's easier for me to spot the signs of trouble!

One word of warning with project managers, and in fact with managers of all types: **don't let non-technical managers take technical decisions!** They will often take bad decisions, through lack of knowledge, that will either come back to bite you immediately or will store up problems for the future.

Project assurance

Project assurance is really just a fancy way of saying that someone is giving guidance to help ensure success.

The role of a project assurance person is to impart skills and experience – direction – to make sure that the project has the maximum chance of staying on the rails and delivering the benefits that you want for your business.

If your project is important, has the potential to deliver big profits, or is costing you a lot of money unless you get it right, why *wouldn't* you want an expert on hand to help give direction and show you what to focus on?

To remind you, a good project assurance person is someone with wide and deep experience of developing software and overseeing successful software delivery. Ideally you want someone with experience as a developer, experience as a project manager, and experience in business and marketing. It can be hard to find a good person for this, but it's worth looking. I've often found, when I perform this role myself, that finding good solutions takes a blend of knowledge from all three areas: software knowledge, project management knowledge, and business knowledge.

It's important to have someone on your project as a sounding board: someone who can answer your questions, someone who you can get second opinions from, a confidant to confide in, someone who can check things like your requirements and specifications to see if they are suitable, and someone to help you do troubleshooting when required. This is especially useful while you are turning the project around, but also has great value in having someone to continue to guide and oversee the project when it is back on track, to make sure that things continue to run smoothly.

Conclusion: What we achieved in step 7

This brings us to the end of the seven-step method for getting your project back on track. People are the most important part of a successful project, but the people you choose depends on the tasks you have to complete. If your budget is tight, just make sure you have at least one highly experienced person, either full-time on your team or performing project assurance to guide you.

Keeping a promise

On the back cover of this book are six bullet points explaining what you will learn from this book. If you've read the book you should now understand what each of those bullet points refers to. That was my promise to you.

If you've read Think and Grow Rich, you'll know that Napoleon Hill refers to a hidden secret in the book—the true formula for success—but he never explicitly reveals it. I'm not going to be that mean to you!

To make sure that I fully deliver on my promise to you, here I will concisely spell out exactly what each of those bullet points on the back cover refers to.

The one true silver bullet for successful software projects

There's only one thing that is proven, time after time, on project after project, to lead to increased success: reducing your scope. Doing less, but doing it better. I cover it in step 2.

The million dollar secret behind keeping your project continually focused on success

A project that succeeds can easily make a million dollars during its lifetime: it only takes $100,000 over 10 years to do this. So, quite simply, the million dollar secret behind keeping your project continually focused on success IS to keep your focus continually on success! You do this by setting clear goals for the project, clearly defining the benefits the project should achieve, clearly communicating them to everyone on the team, and then focusing on continued business justification: consistently measuring and monitoring progress against your goals. This is simple, but so often people get engrossed in the detail and lose sight of the whole point of doing the project in the first place. This is so fundamental that I cover this in step 1.

To get more advanced, consider a formal benefits management framework. The British Computer Society (BCS) now offers the *BCS Professional Certificate in Benefits Planning and Realisation*. It's worth you taking a look at this.

How to piggyback on the knowledge gained from thousands of successful projects

Procter and Gamble marketed a brand of cleaning product called Flash with the advertising slogan, "Flash does the hard work so you don't have to." Sounds good, doesn't it. Fortunately, when it comes to software projects, other people have done the hard work so you don't have to.

Over more than 60 years, thousands of the best and brightest software-minded people have been succeeding, failing, and documenting their methods. Personal Development guru Tony Robbins says "Success leaves clues", and he's exactly right. The knowledge gained has been formalised, written down, and is available for anyone to learn, through books, courses, qualifications, and using the skills of experienced software people.

Throughout this book I've given you the main sources of information to use as a starting point. Sadly they aren't particularly light reading, which is a big opportunity missed by those folks. So if you want to get started using this knowledge immediately, standing on the shoulders of giants, then look for advisors who are skilled in the knowledge and its practical application.

If you only cover one thing yourself in detail, I'd suggest you cover PRINCE2. Get an audio course or video course—the book on its own is perfectly readable but a bit dry.

The 26 major root causes of software project failure... and how to fix them

This is the main bulk of the book. It makes up the entirety of steps 3, 5 and 6. I first explain each point, and then give you a set of action steps that will help you to start tackling these problems.

The #1 personal quality you'll need in order to succeed

I answer this in step 7, with the following:

> The #1 personal quality you'll need in order to succeed is the ability to manage your time so that you have the time to properly focus on the project. Your project will need detailed attention from you and your team to be a success. If you don't have time, delegate to someone and give them authority.

The insider's trick to having software that doesn't suck

I've got one word for you: **testing**. Lots of testing. It's the main difference between good and bad software, between professional projects and disasters. Consider both how the development team tests the software, and how you test the software yourself (User Acceptance Testing).

Most people don't think about testing all that much, scrimp on it, and cut it out when time or money is tight. This is usually a mistake. Compromise on scope (the features the software has) before you compromise on quality (by reducing testing). Otherwise there's not much point in the software having those features anyway, because they won't work properly.

Final Thoughts

I've covered a lot of ground in this book. Admittedly, some of it has been quite superficial, to make sure the book wasn't too long. These days, you can always do a quick Google search on any topics you want more information on, so I thought it was best to give you a general overview of what you need to know, interspersed with some of my own experiences.

Right now, if your project is in a mess, it might be tough to see the way ahead. But I guarantee you, the real problem—the root cause of the mess—is somewhere in this book. You've just got to sniff it out.

Go back to the two lists of *Causes of Failure* at the end of Step 3, and somewhere in that list you'll find your problem.

Then use the knowledge I've given you in the rest of the book to put it right. To help clarify your thinking, sometimes you might just need to take a pen and paper and write down your thoughts. Or, if you keep a journal, ponder on the problem. "Think in ink", as the success speaker Jim Rohn used to say.

Make sure you get to the real root cause of the problem. Each time you find a reason why things are failing, dig further. Keep asking "Why?", over and over again, drilling down further and further into the real root causes of the problem. When you strike bedrock and find that real root cause, it's time to act.

I wish you every success.

INDEX

Symbols

80/20 Principle 94

A

agile 48
Agile Manifesto 55
Agile Principles 53–54
APMP 47, 104
automated testing 117
Axelos 44, 53

B

BDD 115, 116
Behaviour-Driven Development 115
benefits 21, 23, 37, 84
benefits management 142
British Computer Society (BCS) 100
bugs. *See* defects
Business Analyst role 100

C

Camtasia 75
certifications 52
change management 104
commercial off-the-shelf 11, 83, 88
complexity 126
conference calls 106
Confluence, Atlassian 74
continuous delivery 52
continuous deployment 52
core competence 84
cost 27, 31, 32, 37, 84
COTS. *See* Commercial-off-the-shelf

D

Dan Kennedy 64, 94
defect, reproducing 121
defects 39, 61, 62, 87, 114,
        120, 121, 123, 134
demonstrations 105, 108
documentation 73–75

E

estimates 67–69

F

focus groups 64
Fogbugz 123

H

highlight report 45, 66, 67, 72, 108, 125

I

immature technology 109
International Institute of Business
        Analysts (IIBA) 100
International Software Testing Quali-
        fications Board (ISTQB) 137
IT skills problems 39

J

Jim Rohn 144

K

Kanban 50, 93
Kanban board 93

L

lean 53
Lighthouse (software) 123, 125

M

management problems 38
marketing failure 63
meetings 112
Minimum Viable Product (MVP) 52
M_O_R 77
multitasking 91

N

Napoleon Hill 141

O

outdated technology 109

P

planning poker 69
PMBOK 47
PMI 47
PMP 47, 104
PRINCE2 44, 47, 80, 104, 108, 126, 143
PRINCE2 Agile 53
project assurance 46, 61, 102, 110, 112, 115, 127, 129, 137, 139, 140
Project Board 108
project failure 16, 35
project goals 62
project management 38, 42, 138
Project manager 138
proof-of-concept 136

Q

quality 27, 31, 32, 37, 60, 84, 113

R

recruitment 135
regression testing 116
requirements 100
requirements, changing 103–104
requirements checklist 102
resources 84
Return on Investment 36
Return on Investment (ROI) 36
risk 37, 76, 84
risk management 77
risk register 78
risk responses 79, 80
risk threshold 79
root causes of failure 38, 39

S

scope 27, 28, 32, 37, 84, 113, 141
scope diagram 30
screencasts 75
Screenflow (software) 75
Scrum methodology 50, 69
Search Engine Optimization (SEO) 65
security patches 109
Service Level Agreement (SLA) 123
software testing 113
stakeholders 70
stand up meeting 112

sunk cost 83
surveys 105
SWEBOK 133
Sydney Opera House 35

T

technical test 135
test suite 117
Think and Grow Rich 141
time 27, 31, 32, 37, 84
time management 94, 107
Tony Robbins 142
Trello 92

U

Unique Selling Proposition (USP) 64
unit testing 115
Upwork 134
User Acceptance Testing (UAT) 115, 117, 144
user shadowing 105

V

validated learning 52
video 74

W

Whac-A-Mole 124, 125
wiki 74

X

XMind software 29, 118

Y

YAGNI 33

Z

Zendesk software 74